ROMANCING THE BUDDHA

Romancing the Buddha

Embracing Buddhism in My Everyday Life

MICHAEL LISAGOR

MIDDLEWAY

P R E S S

Published by Middleway Press

A division of the SGI-USA

606 Wilshire Blvd., Santa Monica, CA 90401

Copyright 2004 by Michael Lisagor

ISBN 0-9723267-4-X

Design by Gopa & Ted2, Inc.

10   9   8   7   6   5   4   3   2   1

Library of Congress Cataloging-in-Publication Data

Lisagor, Michael.
  Romancing the Buddha / Michael Lisagor.
     p. cm.
  ISBN 0-9723267-4-X (softcover : alk. paper)
  1. Religious life—Soka Gakkai. I. Title.
  BQ8436.2.L57 2005
  294.3'444—dc22

                          2004030768

Contents

Words spoken from the heart have the power to change a person's life. They can even melt the icy walls of mistrust that separate peoples and nations.

—Daisaku Ikeda

Acknowledgments

megan and jamie for being the daughters every father dreams of having • george williams for inspiration • lottie for new beginnings • daisaku ikeda for lighting the way • jeanne for being there • tim for telling me to write • nina for breaking down walls • doris and guy for encouraging us • dave and greg for following through • so many family, friends, fellow buddhists and business associates for never-ending support and kindness • and trude, most beautiful one, you are more than everything I ever wanted

Prologue

. . . .

Fame and momentary glories are no more than illusions.
True happiness lies in cultivating the great state of Buddha-
hood within one's life. This is life's true purpose.
—DAISAKU IKEDA

ROMANCING THE STONE, starring Michael Douglas
and Kathleen Turner, was an adventure-comedy
movie about a hunt for lost treasure in the South American jungles. This book, *Romancing the Buddha*, is an
adventure-comedy story about my hunt for lost treasure in the jungles of urban America and the depths of
my life. Like the poor man in a Buddhist parable who
wandered for years before discovering a priceless jewel
a wealthy friend had sewn into the hem of his robe, I
was unaware of my own Buddha or enlightened nature.
It took considerable personal effort and the guidance
of many sincere teachers for me to begin to live a joy-
ful life.

My parents had very specific opinions on the subject
of treasure. It was anything that conferred status and
wealth. They knew this because their friends had it and
they didn't. Consequently, I grew up equating my self-
worth and success as a human being with my ability to

establish myself in a respected and financially profitable profession.

My older brother decided at an early age to be a dentist. Optometry was to be my chosen career even though I had little interest in it. Still, feigning enthusiasm was much easier than disappointing my parents. But, by the time I was fifteen, I lost even the semblance of caring about being an eye doctor. Since then, I have been engaged in the search for true happiness, the priceless treasure that exists within my own life.

Whether we believe in nature or nurture or both, we can probably agree that in some fashion most of us grew up in dysfunctional families. And, we most likely attended some dysfunctional schools and worked in one or more dysfunctional organizations. So, how do we, as individuals, do more than just survive? How do we have enough time and energy left to enjoy our lives when it takes so much time and energy to overcome our sufferings?

I began practicing Nichiren Buddhism together with my wife in 1969 at the age of nineteen to find the answers to these questions. This book chronicles my thirty-six years of embracing the practice and principles of Buddhism to gradually evolve from a confused and sad teenager into a creative and happy adult, husband and father.

One of the challenges of writing this book was to take into consideration readers who were already familiar with Buddhist concepts and those with little or no knowledge of the subject. Most of the chapters were written over a fifteen-year period for the *World Tribune* newspaper. I have since rewritten them to minimize the use of Buddhist terms and explain the ones I felt were necessary as I related my experiences and perspectives. Still, you might benefit from reading the Brief Introduction to Nichiren Buddhism section prior to enjoying the rest of the book.

Adversity and Personal Growth

Dealing with Adversity

Once you learn how to die, you learn how to live.
—MORRIE SIEGEL FROM *Tuesdays with Morrie*

We've returned from a great summer of '96 family beach vacation and finally finished remodeling the first floor of our house. And even though the Buddhist teachings make it abundantly clear that it is only by overcoming great challenges that I will really grow as a human being, I'm not particularly looking for trouble. So, of course, it finds me instead! Fortunately, as Albert Einstein said, "In the middle of difficulty lies opportunity."

I T'S WEDNESDAY MORNING and as I step out of the shower, I get a little bummed to see the reflection of my shiny bald spot in the not-quite-fogged mirror. I call out for my wife, Trude, to get up and she yells back that her feet are asleep and won't wake up. I start to worry because of her numb-foot episode twelve years ago that had us all concerned even though it turned out to be a temporary spinal disk problem.

Trude goes to school; she teaches sixth grade. I go to work and we both keep our Buddhist fingers crossed.

Thursday morning Trude wakes up numb from the

waist down. Can't feel a thing. Doesn't seem to affect her bodily functions and strength—she just isn't receiving any sensations. A million thoughts run through my mind—worries—nightmare scenarios too depressing to mention.

Our family physician is on call and sees us right away. She sends us to a neurologist who orders an MRI and suggests a spinal tap the following Monday.

Now it's Friday morning and Trude can barely walk. It's breaking my heart. In twenty-seven years, I've never seen her so vulnerable and scared. She has been my pillar, my source of strength. It's Mike who gets the strange illnesses—it's Mike who catches chicken pox from the girls and almost dies. Trude just keeps on truckin'—why, she's indestructible! Or so it seemed.

We rush to the neurologist again. Trude almost falls while walking on her tiptoes for him and barely avoids hurting her ankle. I'm trying to be strong but want to cry. While she lies in the MRI chamber, I sit outside in my car for an hour chanting Nam-myoho-renge-kyo, the phrase Nichiren Buddhists chant every day.

Through his exhaustive studies and internal realizations in turbulent thirteenth-century Japan, the Buddhist monk Nichiren came to realize that Myoho-renge-kyo, the title of the Lotus Sutra, a written record of the teachings of the first recorded Buddha, Shakyamuni, was actually the essence of that sutra's teaching. Nichiren was able to concentrate all these profound lessons into one simple but profound phrase that enabled people to attain Buddhahood —their fundamental identity as an enlightened being. Adding the word *nam* for "devotion to," Nichiren gave us a tangible means to express our enlightenment in everyday life. By saying the words *Nam-myoho-renge-kyo* out loud, we are able to tap into our inner wisdom, compassion and joy. This positive inner change then reflects in dramatic improvements in our surroundings.

I realize that even in the midst of this unknown illness, Trude is incredibly strong. At home, we sit together and do our Buddhist prayers. We each silently express our appreciation for the functions in our life and environment that protect us. Nichiren Buddhism is based on the reality that our surroundings are a reflection of our life. Through chanting and then taking action, we can manifest our enlightenment. This causes both conspicuous and inconspicuous improvements in our environment in the same way our shadow straightens when we stand up. Some philosophers have likened this process to returning to our spiritual center. Our Buddhism refers to this process of inner transformation as individual human revolution.

One of the interpretations of the word *kyo* is harmony. When we chant, we are more in rhythm with our environment—things seem to go our way more often. Nichiren explained that a true life philosophy should not only be historically and theoretically sound but also must provide actual proof in the lives of its believers. Needless to say, we offer intense prayers for actual proof.

At one point during our prayers, I sincerely ask Trude what she thinks I should pray for. She says, a twinkle in her eye, "Well, Mike, how about a pony?" I look shocked. She sings, her arms waving back and forth, "A pony or Trude's health? A pony or Trude's health?" We fall together laughing and then begin to chant.

Nothing conclusive is learned from the MRI. The good news is she doesn't have a tumor or a major back problem. But she could have multiple sclerosis or Lyme disease or who knows what.

The doctor is very warm and patient. He has us check Trude into the hospital for a spinal tap that evening. At home, while we're packing, our youngest daughter, Jamie, is finding her special pajamas to loan Mom, while Trude and I hug each other and finally have a much needed cry. We know we'll get through this, but we're still frightened.

Things like this happen to other people. We've lost my sister, mother and father and Trude's father, so we're not strangers to hospitals and serious illnesses. But this is so different; this is the woman I love more than anyone or anything in the world. This is my karmic mate—we've chanted together almost every day for twenty-seven years. We've agreed to find each other again in the next lifetime (although I had to promise to do the grocery shopping!).

Nichiren Buddhism explains that there is an ultimate realm within our life called *amala*-consciousness or enlightenment. This place in our life is connected with the life of the universe, Nam-myoho-renge-kyo, the ultimate Law of life and death. So both life and death are natural expressions of human existence. By basing our beliefs and actions on the great universal life of Buddhahood that exists within the depths of our lives, we can face death with dignity and peace. Nichiren explained that by chanting Nam-myoho-renge-kyo, we experience a surge of joy and, eventually, overcome our fear of death. Then we can begin to focus our lives on helping others.

Eternity is an elusive concept. How do I conceive of a time without beginning or end? Still, I've come to accept that my life is at some level connected to everyone else in the world and believe that this relationship extends for generations backward and forward into the future. Maybe it is related to the "butterfly effect" physicists describe—that a seemingly random event in one part of the world often causes significant changes elsewhere. I like to think that every time I manage to perform a compassionate act, it causes ripples across the universe.

Jamie calls family and friends to tell them about her mother. A year later in her college entrance essay, she revealed how difficult it was for her to deliver this news—how she found herself having to encourage everyone else when she herself was silently crying out for comfort.

From the car, we phone her older sister, Megan, who is away at the University of Virginia. It's a real challenge to make sure she knows what's going on without freaking her out. We have always been honest with our children. So it is important to communicate clearly to her exactly what we know and don't know about Trude's sudden illness since it is often emotionally difficult to accept that "no news" is not "good news or bad news" but merely "no news."

We check Trude into her hospital room without any hassle. Trude has me arrange all her things just so…some habits die hard. When I return from talking to the nurse, the doctor is in her room taking some fluid out of her spine. We've heard this is a terrible procedure, but it didn't hurt too much (easy for me to say) and Trude stayed on her stomach for two hours just like she was supposed to; she didn't suffer any headaches or other dreaded side effects.

It's very hard leaving Trude that night. She looks so alone and disoriented. I pretty much cry and chant all the way home. Trude mentioned to me that she was glad our faith was such that we never questioned why this was happening to us. We both understand that this is our time to advance in our practice and prove the limitless power of Nam-myoho-renge-kyo—to bring forth from within our lives the power to heal. As my friend, Jeff, likes to say, "Suffering unlocks the door to our Buddha nature."

The next few days are, I think, the most difficult I've ever experienced. I'm emotionally and physically exhausted. I always wondered how I would react if my spouse had a debilitating illness. Would I panic? Run away? Lose my confidence? I'm really pleased to discover that, with a lot of help from my practice, I can do whatever is needed. And also that the love I have for this woman really does know no limits. Our daughter, Megan, comes home from college overnight and entertains us with funny stories as only she can.

> *If one's illness is caused by fixed karma, even excellent medicine will turn to poison, but that, if one believes in the Lotus Sutra, poison will change into medicine.*
> —NICHIREN

After the first day in the hospital, the nurses and doctors decide to put Trude in a private room, at no additional cost, so she can rest. She can freely chant whenever she wants. Numerous precious friends visit her. Trude strolls around the hallways with her walker in her colorful pajamas greeting nurses and patients, trying to encourage them.

An old friend, one of the first people in the United States to practice Nichiren Buddhism, calls Trude to see how she is doing. We have a picture of our oldest daughter as a baby in his arms from many years ago in Los Angeles. Just hearing his vigorous, confident voice penetrates Trude's life like an arrow. She can't stay on the phone since the neurologist comes in to tell her that some kind of virus has invaded her spine and there is no way of knowing how damaged her nerves are.

When Trude calls our friend back, he reminds her that the doctors, while sincerely trying to help her, are still outside her. Only Nam-myoho-renge-kyo is actually inside her life and so can affect everything. Trude shares this with me, and we really become determined to achieve a great victory. After six days in the hospital and extensive steroid intravenous treatments to counter the inflammation, she comes home to physical therapy and chanting.

> *Life is a struggle with ourselves. It is a tug-of-war between moving forward and regressing, between happiness and unhappiness.*
> —DAISAKU IKEDA

It's now three weeks later and Trude is still in physical therapy. She has begun to regain some feeling in her feet and knees and her spirits are incredibly high. Although someone who wants to be in control of her life, she is for the first time forced to allow others to help her and express their love. Teachers from her school cook us meals; her former students from the last ten years circulate a get well card to the local high schools and present their wishes for her speedy recovery.

She makes a major breakthrough in communication and trust with her mother. She also verbalizes a new awareness of her purpose in life as something beyond (in addition to) her role as a mother, wife and teacher. Her medicine keeps her up at night, so she begins writing a journal of her struggle and the changes she goes through—she is already on page 105. It helps her focus her thoughts when she encourages the many people who call and visit her. This remarkable woman is changing in so many ways!

This story has no real ending. It's our life…it's the joys and sorrows we need to experience to transform our inner lives, what we call human revolution, and manifest our enlightened nature. I'm confident that given time, Trude's nerves will heal and we will eventually receive a definitive diagnosis. But, more important, we both now have a much deeper appreciation for our lives, for each other and for the treasure that is Nichiren Buddhism.

Buddhism and Psychotherapy

By 1997, the permanency of Trude's illness coupled with another tragic event in my life threatens to emotionally overwhelm me. I've taken a job as the vice president of business development at an information technology company in Northern Virginia. Our daughter, Jamie, has started Rice University in Houston, and her older sister, Megan, is in her fourth year at the University of Virginia.

UNTIL THE SUMMER of 1997, I wasn't particularly open-minded on the subject of psychotherapy. I would meet people who were seeing a therapist and think to myself, "This isn't for me. They're spending too much time dwelling on the past rather than changing their karma and making causes for the future."

Buddhism expounds the law of cause and effect that operates in life, ranging over past, present and future existences. This causality underlies the doctrine of karma. From this viewpoint, causes formed in the past are manifested as effects in the present. Causes formed in the present will be manifested as effects in the future. Buddhism emphasizes the causes one creates and accumulates in the present, because these will determine one's future.

Unfortunately, I believed that seeking the services of a therapist would be a sign of weakness rather than a meaningful cause for my future. I was also concerned how others might react. If I were to see a therapist, I thought I would be in essence admitting to myself that Buddhism didn't have the power to change my life or that my faith was too weak.

My many years of daily Buddhist practice had enabled me to gain a large degree of control over my negative thoughts and I was much happier with myself. I had learned that if I chanted a lot, I could make my mind quiet down enough for me to function in daily life. I was also able to make and carry out strong determinations, have a warm, loving family and build a very successful business career. Still, though I had overcome much of my unhappiness and insecurity through chanting, I was never entirely without the underlying sadness and frustration that had tugged at me since my childhood.

What I began to realize was that, through my Buddhist practice, I had finally opened up enough to begin to explore some very painful aspects of my life. In his letter "The Strategy of the Lotus Sutra," Nichiren said, "Employ the strategy of the Lotus Sutra before any other."

In this letter, Nichiren explained the importance of putting our faith first when facing a serious challenge. However, he didn't say we shouldn't seek out the appropriate medicine and guidance to heal ourselves but that we should base these activities on the wisdom derived from our Buddhist practice. This realization helped change my attitude about therapy. At this point, all I needed was a powerful catalyst, an event that would compel me to seek help. Soon, two traumatic occurrences pushed me right over the edge and into therapy.

The first was the suicide of my good friend, Gordon. He had been my business mentor and a source of inspiration for most of the seventies and had recently retired. His family and friends thought they knew him very well. He was always cheerful and full of great advice. It frightened me that he could be harboring such overwhelming anguish that he saw no way to continue living. Obviously, he hadn't dealt with many of the issues in his life. I wondered if I was in danger of making the same mistake.

A few years later, Trude was diagnosed with multiple sclerosis. For the first six months, we both focused on finding the benefit of her illness. We gained a deeper appreciation for our practice, friends and each other as well as a stronger sense of purpose. We looked at the gain but had yet to face the loss in our lives. One evening in 1998, Trude discovered me lying down almost comatose, unable to move. I had fallen into an extremely depressed state, the kind of loneliness and helplessness I had experienced as a child and teenager. I was clearly in need of help.

There have been numerous leaders in our Buddhist community over the years who have greatly encouraged and inspired me in my practice. However, it was through the additional help of a therapist, Jeanne, that I was finally able to begin the painful but rewarding process of healing myself from the effects of my childhood, so that I could truly devote myself to the present. So in the same way Trude went to a neurologist for her illness, I went to a psychotherapist for mine.

Jeanne had studied Buddhist philosophy and meditation for many years and so was readily able to relate to my practice. Starting with my tremendous fear of losing Trude, I began to explore other aspects of my life that I had previously been too afraid to face.

This was not an easy process. I had to push myself through many tears and painful memories. I discovered that the messages I had assimilated as a child from an angry and abusive father and a disinterested mother had greatly influenced my opinion of myself. As an adult, many of my actions continued to reflect these childhood impressions. The behaviors that protected me as a child were no longer necessary or desirable.

When I was a child, my family moved every few years to a new city. As the perpetual new student, I learned how to hide behind a wall of humor and sarcasm. This was my way of avoiding the inevitable hurt of separation. During this time I also became very depressed—a dark inner atmosphere that would haunt me for many years.

We had little discourse in our family. We usually ate our frozen dinners on metal trays while watching television.

My early memories of the late fifties and early sixties center on scenes on our old television of news events, Ed Sullivan and Disney's *The Wonderful World of Color*. Most of my intellectual and spiritual upbringing came from books. I spent hundreds of hours reading biographies and wishing that I could just close my eyes and become someone else…someone in control of his life, able to really function in society. This yearning and frustration stayed with me throughout my teen years as I experimented with drugs and ran away from home with my future wife. Eventually, my sadness motivated me to begin practicing Nichiren Buddhism in 1969.

I've learned that every child wants a million dollars of effective parenting from their mother and father. Unfortunately, not too many parents have that much to give. Mine could barely manage a few thousand! Eventually, Buddhism and therapy became about learning how to parent my inner self. As I romanced the Buddha in my life, I started to learn how to forgive adolescent me and rely more on enlightened me.

Over the course of three years of counseling, I came to realize that psychotherapy was an answer to my Buddhist prayers. Perhaps Nichiren could be considered a therapist! Understanding that human beings are often deluded, he often emphasized that a person must "become the master of your mind rather than let your mind master you." The same lessons I was learning from Nichiren's letters from a spiritual perspective were consistent with the realizations I was having on a more personal level through psychotherapy. Some of these were: understanding the difference between feeling obligated to do something and choosing to do something; allowing myself to enjoy life without feeling guilty about it; accepting that none of my attachments to people or things in this life will last forever; and acknowledging that it isn't necessary to be busy, or worried or like someone else to be deserving of respect.

For many years, Trude and I have chanted side by side. We like to think this has contributed to the strong love and unity in our family. We decided to chant even more to make significant progress in every aspect of our lives including extracting the most possible benefit from my therapy.

The ever-present heaviness that had plagued me has now diminished significantly. There is no way to describe how wonderful this makes me feel. I am also learning to allow myself to feel joy without guilt and to experience pain without panic. The essence of this is being able to live in the moment—something we are taught as Buddhists but that can be very elusive.

I don't feel that psychotherapy has in any way diminished my faith in Nichiren Buddhism. Rather, it has enhanced my practice. I am able to sit quietly and concentrate on my prayers where before I had a difficult time focusing for more than a few minutes at a time. Accepting that the emotions I'm feeling do not always reflect the truth, and that they won't last forever, has helped me develop a more stable spiritual foundation. I am also learning new habits, new ways of thinking. My chanting has accelerated and strengthened this process. I am slowly overcoming my addiction to drama and constant turmoil, an obsession with being busy and a belief that I have to be funny for people to like me.

With my Buddhist practice as the prime point of my personal development, therapy has played an important supportive role, much as my wife challenges her illness with chanting and the help of medical professionals.

I now have a much more profound appreciation and respect for anyone who takes constructive steps toward increased self-awareness and self-improvement. I also believe these actions are consistent with a Buddhist practice. The key isn't whether something has a socially acceptable label but whether it rings true. And each of us must judge that for ourselves.

A Major Shot of Hope

....

This dialogue is the third in a series of experiences about the incredible personal growth our family experienced through dealing with my wife's illness.

> *No matter what happens, please continue to chant Nam-myoho-renge-kyo—in both good times and bad, unswayed by joys or sorrows, happiness or suffering. Then you will be able to seize victory in daily life and in society.*
> —DAISAKU IKEDA

Trude: In April 2001, I walked six miles to raise money for multiple sclerosis research. What makes this noteworthy is that just five years before, I couldn't walk at all.

Mike: It usually takes a crisis to propel me to undergo significant personal growth. When we learned that Trude had MS, I was filled with a deep sense of loss for Trude, our two daughters and me. Looking back five years later, I can hardly believe how many areas of our lives have positively developed as a result of this terrible illness.

Trude: MS entered my life at tornado speed in September 1996. In just three days, my symptoms progressed from the tingly feeling of my feet falling asleep to an overwhelming numbness from my waist down. A week in the hospital, slowly relearning to walk, reassuring my two daughters I was okay and, finally, the disturbing diagnosis of multiple sclerosis caught me—the always healthy, independent, in control and seemingly invincible woman—totally by surprise. One of my early journal entries written from my hospital bed reads: "Mike called when I was in the middle of chanting and all of a sudden I started crying uncontrollably. It shocks me how that happens, but we eventually returned to our conversation and it seemed like he rode the river successfully with me and knew he was an important part of the ride. I'm just not a person who has emotional outbursts or at least I wasn't that way before. So many questions are coursing through me—some profound, others rather mundane. Still, I really felt the underlying spiritual strength from twenty-seven years of chanting together."

Mike: I watched Trude challenge her situation with astonishing determination both in terms of chanting for her spirit and going to physical therapy for her recalcitrant limbs. And something new for Ms. Solid as a Rock, she allowed herself to be helped by everyone around her. Fellow teachers took turns bringing over dinners while Buddhist friends chanted with Trude for hours during the day. For my part, I discovered that when push came to shove, I was able to stand on my own and be strong for her. With the help of this remarkable practice and a compassionate therapist, I turned what could have been a devastating occurrence into the fuel to make personal changes that had continued to elude me, including being able to face and overcome my childhood sadness and anger. Meanwhile, my love and admiration for Trude and my appreciation that I am able to chant each day continue to grow.

> *I find that if I am thinking too much of my own problems and the fact that at times things are not just like I want them to be, I do not make any progress at all. But if I look around and see what I can do, and then I do it, I move on.*
> —ROSA PARKS FROM *Quiet Strength*

Trude: Medical researchers recently confirmed that Avonex, a beta interferon drug, has shown dramatic results for patients with relapse-remitting multiple sclerosis. Of course, I didn't know this when I made the difficult decision to begin Avonex several years ago. Perhaps to a fault, I had always avoided taking medication—I'd simply will colds and headaches away. Now my neurologist was proposing I take a weekly injection that wasn't a cure but was possibly a way to increase the time between relapses. My long list of questions could not be adequately answered. Yet, ultimately, the decision was mine to make. In an effort to clarify matters, I went for a second opinion but this doctor said he was "on the fence."

On the drive home, we called one of our fellow Buddhists. I expressed to him my concern that I should be able to overcome this illness solely through my practice. He didn't try to tell me what to do but reminded me that through my practice, I would gain the wisdom to understand what action to take. And, deciding to take the medication wouldn't mean my faith was weak. In the end, after many hours of chanting and my determination to make causes to improve my health, I decided to start taking the shots. Since that time, I've seen a continued improvement in my health.

Mike: For the first few years, Trude couldn't walk any substantial distances. Then we decided to start walking regularly in preparation for the MS Walk. This made a real difference in Trude's health and stamina. And there were a lot of tears when she crossed the finish line.

Trude: Mike and I recently moved from Virginia to beautiful Bainbridge Island, Washington, where the weather is much more suitable for someone with MS.

Before we left, we gathered almost a hundred of our family, co-workers, clients and friends and raised five thousand dollars for MS research. This was a great opportunity for us to take concrete action as Nichiren Buddhists in our community.

It was up to me to transform this unexpected setback

in my life into a source of personal growth and victory. Because of the support of my family, friends and doc-tors, my life is much richer than ever before. This experience has deepened my compassion for others. As for the injections, my minor weekly stab of pain has become a major shot of hope.

The Early Morning Blues

. . . . ·..

Or How to Transform Life's Poisons into Medicines and
Become an Obnoxiously Cheerful Morning Person

WHEN I WAS YOUNGER, getting up early in the morning was never an issue. I just didn't do it! It was obvious to me that when ol' Ben Franklin scribed the famous words "early to bed and early to rise," he meant crawling into bed sometime after midnight and being dragged out of bed several hours after the sun. Now, many years later, I can associate my inability to get up with what Nichiren Buddhism terms the three poisons: greed, anger and foolishness. I was greedy for more sleep, angry with anyone who tried to wake me and too stupid to realize why I should get up.

One of my most awful oversleeping experiences occurred in the early seventies. I had been married for just a few years. Trude was doing some serious reflecting on how far love would carry us in our relationship considering I was still fairly irresponsible in the daily life department. My idea of common sense was driving on the right side of the road when returning from visiting friends after midnight. Somehow, having to get up early for work just didn't seem very relevant the night before.

One morning, knowing I was a late sleeper, Trude forced me out of bed, chanted with me, fed me and then sent me off in my old Volkswagen to my job as a circuit designer at a small company in Chatsworth, California. She was, I'm sure, confident that I would keep this job at least another week. Unfortunately, she had her own job and couldn't follow me to work. Upon reaching the parking lot, I fell back asleep in my car. My supervisor actually had to come outside to fire me! I wish I could tell you how humiliating that was, but I was pretty tired at the time and don't remember much of what happened.

Eventually, I concluded that the real secret to getting up in the morning was to learn to enjoy my daily life— to have a real reason to get up. That realization took quite a few years to actually put into practice.

It was very encouraging to me, being relatively young, that one of my older friends, a man I respected, also had a difficult time waking up. He invented some rather interesting ways to wake himself, including perhaps the loudest stereo music ever played in Santa Monica, California. Thanks to him, his neighbors got to work on time. They had no choice.

Unfortunately, he slept right through the music. I'm pretty sure he eventually overcame his early morning blues, since I have seen him awake on numerous occasions at early morning meetings.

I can't honestly say that learning to get up on time happened overnight. I didn't just wake up one morning and exclaim, "I'm healed! I'll never oversleep again." Rather, it was a painfully slow struggle against my laziness that spanned several years.

I've tried numerous tricks to wake myself up. Once, I overfilled our waterbed, thinking that a firmer bed would be less comfortable in the morning. I also set our clock to tell the incorrect time, so when the red LEDs flashed six o'clock, it was really only five-thirty. Of course, I would just hit the snooze alarm but the appearance of thirty extra minutes of sleep seemed to help.

The only "trick" that has really worked has been to continue to develop my life. Each year, as my jobs improved and my depression lessened, I had less and less trouble rising. I started having a stronger sense of responsibility about going to work and also recognized the importance of starting the day with a strong Buddhist practice.

I now always get up on time. (Really, I do!) I used my practice to turn the three poisons of greed, anger and foolishness into a healthier, more balanced lifestyle. My greed or desire for sleep was overtaken by the need to become a responsible husband and father, to share the benefits of hard work with my family and friends. My anger at others and society for "forcing me to have to work" was replaced with anger at myself for not taking the responsibility for my own happiness.

Coupled with a growing confidence in myself, I was able to change my poor attitude about work. Finally, instead of seeking to find value outside myself, always wishing for elusive overnight fame and fortune, I put aside such foolishness and gained the wisdom necessary to start taking small day-by-day steps toward my happiness.

This doesn't seem so profound now that I'm rereading it. But coming from a life fairly devoid of happiness to being able to wake up each morning looking forward to my day truly astounds me. I do feel the need to add the following disclaimer, especially to fathers. An unfortunate by-product of this life transformation is the tendency to become an obnoxiously cheerful morning person. I sing in the bathroom. I dance in the closet. I whistle in the kitchen. This behavior really irritates my daughters. I've tried to stop, but I'm usually not even aware I'm doing it. Maybe I'm channeling for a sixties rock group.

Of course, I entirely empathize with their feelings. They play hard, study hard and need lots of sleep. Days and days of sleep. They store up sleep molecules like chipmunks store nuts. They don't pop out of bed in the morning, they crawl. The only energy they exhibit is to yell, "Five more minutes!" or "It's her turn; I got up first yesterday!" They mosey around like alligators and, if I happen to be humming nearby, bite my head off. But I don't really mind. After all, I totally love them and, deep down, even if they don't realize it now, they would be much angrier with me if I lost my job for oversleeping.

But I thought I'd warn you anyway.

Family and Relationships

Thoughts on Marriage

....

The ultimately important thing is for both partners to decide resolutely to make the marriage work by allowing love to permeate their beings and their mental attitudes to the extent that they are open to each other for the sake of mutual assistance and growth. Honesty, communication and dialogue are called for. The tremendous challenge involved in achieving such openness reminds us that love is not merely a promise or an entitlement. To bear fruit, it must be created and recreated over and over. That is the only way to solve the many problems we all encounter in marriage.

—JOHAN GALTUNG FROM *Choose Peace*

M Y MARRIAGE had a rocky start. We ran away from home in 1969, the day my wife graduated high school, and started our Buddhist practice a few months later. Most Beautiful One (not Trude's real name) and I loved each other intensely. But at just eighteen and nineteen years old, we lacked vital communication skills. I struggled with depression and she struggled with me struggling with depression. Activities most people took for granted, like working an eight-hour day, were beyond my emotional grasp.

We also had a difficult time getting along. I was in the Soka Gakkai International — our Buddhist community of more than twelve million lay practitioners — marching band in the early seventies and Most Beautiful One was on the drill team. Every Sunday after marching practice we stopped by the same Buddhist friend's house at different times to complain about each other. I thought she was too judgmental and she was tired of me being so irresponsible. We definitely weren't seeing the Buddha or enlightened nature in each other. The advice he gave us was basically this: as long as we blamed each other for our problems, we would never be happy. He also said that rather than facing each other, we should sit side by side as we chant and face our enlightened selves, which are mirrored in the mandala, called a Gohonzon, Nichiren Buddhists chant to each day. What followed has been a thirty-six-year journey of chanting every day to polish our enlightened natures, overcoming numerous obstacles and consistently working to improve our relationship. The result has been an absolutely wonderful life together.

In 2003, we were asked to speak at our older daughter's friend's wedding ceremony at a stately old mansion in the western part of Virginia. It took us two weeks of reflection and dialogue to describe some of the lessons we've learned about marriage. Here's what we shared:

Communicate...set aside a regular time to talk,

But be flexible and willing to listen regardless of the time.

Recognize and accommodate your different communication styles.

Don't go to bed angry, even if it means losing sleep to discussion.

Give your relationship constant attention.

Enjoy the good times.

Realize life's challenges will cause you to grow and deepen your bond.

Reach out to help others...it makes your own burdens seem lighter.

Love deeply and passionately.

Always keep your sense of humor.

Laugh together.

Celebrate each other's strengths.

Reflect on your own weaknesses.

Respect each other.

Act with compassion when your spouse is struggling.

Spend quality time together.

Yet give each other space to develop as individuals... it will make the time you spend together more fulfilling.

Remember that spiritual growth is a key component of a happy, life-long marriage...all the money,

Recognition and status in the world won't guarantee happiness.

Your marriage is truly a treasure.

And so are both of you!

Most Beautiful One and I have spent many years working on improving our relationship. After we had our second daughter, someone pointed out to us that children learn much more about relationships from watching how their parents treat each other than from what parents tell them. I am thankful that both the girls have grown up expecting to be treated with respect and dignity.

The unity between parents is also vitally important. Along with our Buddhist practice, we have always tried to put our relationship first. To do this, we've had to learn to transform our anger at the other person's behavior into dialogue about self-improvement. I've also had to learn to trust my wife to fix her own problems — that I don't have to fix them for her.

As a result of these realizations, we've been able to turn our disagreements and external challenges into continual growth in our relationship. The goal of our marriage, as we see it, is to become closer and closer to each other and to share that closeness with others. Our love and chanting Nam-myoho-renge-kyo are the glue that helps us stick together. It's important to romance the Buddha not just in ourselves but in those around us.

Teenagers Are Aliens

....

A little nonsense now and then is relished by the wisest men.
—ROALD DAHL FROM *Charlie and the Chocolate Factory*

I've CHANGED THE NAMES of my daughters and wife in this essay to avoid embarrassing them. The role of Jamie at the age of fourteen is portrayed by a fictional character named Jaye. Megan at the age of seventeen is disguised as Meg. Trude, my wife, is referred to as Most Beautiful One. The year is 1994 and the girls are in junior high and high school. Trude is teaching sixth grade and I'm a marketing director at an information technology company and just finishing a master's degree program.

A teenager is a humanoid creature from another planet. Ha, just kidding. A teenager is a permanent alien visitor in an otherwise hormonally balanced household who drives, communicates telephonically, thinks Smashing Pumpkins is a musical group and has friends whose parents never seem to feed them dinner so they eat everything in our refrigerator.

"Teenagehood," I was assured by my more elderly, experienced friends, was a time to be dreaded, like the plague. I was filled with images of my daughters becoming mutant ninja android Friday-the-thirteenth creatures whose only purpose in life was to torture their mother and me. I'm pleased to be able to report that these fears were groundless. However, the teenage years were not without challenges. So, in the spirit of "helping others" journalism, here are some lessons learned for future parents of teenagers.

Sports.

I should have purchased stock in the local orthopedic medical office. Based on my younger daughter's experience, I would have made a bundle. An example:

(Tuesday, eleven o'clock in the evening)

Ring-a-ding. A sleepy "Hello?"

"Is this Most Beautiful One?"

"Yes. Who is this?"

"This is Mr. Thomas, Jaye's coach. I'm calling from soccer camp in West Virginia and, even though we're at the emergency hospital, Jaye is not too seriously injured."

Sharp elbow on my side. "Mike, wake up."

"Who is it?"

"Mr. Thomas."

"Why would I want an English muffin this late at night?"

"No, Jaye's soccer coach."

"Is she late for practice?"

"No, she's hurt. She's in the hospital."

"What's her coach doing in the hospital?"

"Never mind, Mike."

Jaye, it turned out, in a moment of unusual (for her) psycho-aggression, placed herself in front of an opposing team's forward (eight hundred pounds, eight feet six inches) who was preparing to kick the ball into Tennessee. Instead, the girl drilled it (the ball, not the state) into Jaye's rib cage. Jaye's coach, knowing he wouldn't have to pay any future hospital bills, immediately assigned her a new nickname—Tiger. Just what I needed—an injury-prone daughter with the moniker Tiger.

"It hurts when I laugh, Dad."

"Well, maybe you should chant more consistently this summer like you did during the school year."

"But, it hurts when I chant, Dad."

"Well, maybe you should play a non-contact sport like reading."

"But I love soccer."

"You spend a lot of time in casts."

"Didn't you tell me to challenge myself?"

Jaye, a new high-school freshman, had expressed an interest in field hockey. I offered to hit her in the head with her hockey stick, thus sparing her a semester of after-school practices and more serious injuries.

"Not funny," she declared.

Nichiren Buddhism explains that each human being has his or her own unique karma and, therefore, unique mission in this life. So while parents should try to set a good example for their children and provide them with thoughtful guidance, we each have to step back and allow them to face their own challenges... make their own mistakes so that they can learn and grow as human beings. One of the most emotionally difficult aspects of being the parent of a teenager is knowing when to step in and when to let go.

Curfew.

Many of my older daughter Meg's friends have curfews. A curfew is a specific time established by parental authority figures so the parents can get a good night's sleep without wondering where their teenagers are between the hours of, say, midnight and next year. Much to other parents' amazement, our daughter had no curfew. Why, you ask?

a.   Because we trust her judgment.
b.   She's much smarter than we were at that age.
c.   She probably won't do anything worse than we did.
d.   All of the above.

The correct answer is d. We did have an agreed-upon time on weekend evenings that she had to call to let us know that she was alive, that she did not elope with an armed radical urban warrior and the time she would be home. We lay awake in bed waiting for this call. She thought this was pretty funny. Of course, she also thought it was pretty funny that I was losing most of my hair. Someday, we told her, you might have a teenage child and a balding husband and then your concept of humor will change. She thought that was hysterical.

The telephone.

If I had a therapist back then, I'm sure she would have attributed my inferiority complex to the fact that forty-seven of every fifty phone calls at our house were for my daughters. The phone never used to ring for Most Beautiful One and me. We received our calls, actually messages, via call waiting. "Can my Dad call you back in a few minutes, Mr. President? I'm on the other line with a friend."

Parents should respect the privacy of their children and not listen in on their personal conversations. But do you have any idea how frustrating it is to hear:

"She did what with whom? Oh, my God! Well, you know I actually…" (Interruption followed by:)

"Dad, will you hang up the phone? I'm taking it upstairs."

I did some fairly advanced research on the relationship between teenagers and their telephone habits. Jaye left her things—soccer shoes, homework and spaceships—all over the house. During a typical phone conversation, she wandered from room to room searching for something without hanging up the previous receiver.

Our family used to spend hours scouring the house for the off-the-hook phone.

Meg, on the other hand, viewed the transmitter as the conversational equivalent of a bullhorn. It is no coincidence that this is now referred to in some circles as a meg-a-phone. I once overheard her talking excitedly about something that happened at school while driving my car over two miles away. (She doesn't realize it, but I still hear all her secrets even when she hides in her old bedroom with the portable phone.) Rats! She just read this. Now she's in the guest bathroom talking to her friend with the fan running.

Nagging.

Teenagers should be proud. After all, they are the hope for the future of humankind. But also they serve a vital function in society today—they give us parents countless things to complain about.

Nagging children is an art. But like any creative endeavor, it can be overdone. (At least I think so.) Both Meg and Jaye learned to roll their eyes, truly a future career-enhancing ability, as a result of my constant reminder to remove their clothes from our bathroom floor and their mother's weekly "put away your laundry." It had taken twenty-five years for Most Beautiful One to transform me from a teenage slob into a neat and tidy person. So while I wholeheartedly believed a father should share 100 percent of all parental responsibilities, I drew the line at nagging about neatness. Entering Jaye's room at night was a mystical journey back to my own messy childhood. It took up to twenty minutes to find her. I loved it! Anyway, we tried not to pester our kids too much, but hey, no one's perfect.

Peer pressure.

Most Beautiful One and I had dinner with two of our closest friends, John and Mary (not Tim and Nina's real names). In 1994, they had already known our family for twelve years. We discussed the tremendous peer pressures faced by our children. They were surrounded by other youth engaged in many types of nonproductive behavior. Our friends remarked that they had seen the positive influence of our Buddhist practice on our family values. They believed this provided Meg and Jaye with the self-confidence necessary to make wise judgments both in the people they associated with and the types of activities they engaged in. Now that they are both in their twenties, I can see that this was definitely the case. Meg and Jaye both have well-developed self-images. This has given them the confidence to make fun of me on a daily basis.

They are also aware of the importance of the spiritual side of their lives. It is clear to me that to be effective, a religion must not be so restrictive that it refuses to encourage a respect for diversity and open-mindedness in young people. It also must enable individuals to take constructive action toward their own happiness and the advancement of peace.

In his book, *The Way of Youth*, Daisaku Ikeda said, "I have made it one of my aims to help young people to have hope and confidence in their future. I myself have infinite trust in young people, and so I say to them: You are the hope of humanity! Each of you has a bright future ahead. Each of you has a precious potential waiting to be developed. Your success, your victory will be a victory for all of us. Your victory will lead the way in this century, the century of peace and humanity, the most important century for all humankind."

Fortunately, parents don't have to be perfect. But children—even teenagers—do watch what their parents do as opposed to what they say. It's always been more important for me to challenge my own life and continue to strive to do my human revolution than to lecture my daughters on what they should be doing. We need to show our children that they can make a positive impact on the world. That's the real challenge of being a parent. And setting the example is the best way to accomplish this...at least until our children return to their home planet!

To My Daughters

....

Two words I would never associate with my childhood are "com-passion" and "encouragement." In 1999, on Father's Day, I wrote a letter that expresses the guidance and love I wish I had received from my father. (He passed away several years ago.) The act of writing the letter was a very healing process.

Fortunately, I have a much healthier, loving relationship with my own two daughters. My older, soon-to-be-married daughter is a journalist. My younger daughter is just finishing law school. They are both remarkable young adults. I decided to give them a similar letter as a reminder of some of life's important lessons as well as a way to tell them one more time that no matter what may happen in their lives, they are truly loved. This, I believe, is the greatest gift a parent has to give.

Dear Megan and Jamie:
Here are some guidelines...rules of the road I would like to share with the two most wonderful daughters in the world.

Never forget that you are always loved. No matter what you do or where you go or what mistakes you make, Mom and I will always love you. Follow your own heart and do what you want to with your life, not what other people think you should do.

Learn to accept your joys and your sorrows. Through your sorrows you will grow and learn valuable lessons about life and yourself. Your joys will cause you to reflect on the mystery and beauty of life. Sorrows will make the joys even sweeter. It's okay to be sad sometimes. No one will think less of you. Don't hide your sadness…you might not be able to find it when you need to. It's okay to let another person comfort you. Going through your own hardships will then enable you to comfort others.

Face your fears. When you're afraid, find someone you can talk to and trust. Some of your fears are justified and serve to protect you from real harm. But most of them will prevent you from expanding your life. More often than not, your greatest fears are in your imagination and don't exist in reality. Recognize your nightmares as just fears in technicolor. Observe them as you would a horror movie. Be scared but don't let your fears paralyze you. If all else fails, come to me for a hug. Even if it's in the middle of the night. I'll always have time for you.

Don't be afraid to dream big. The sky's the limit. You won't be able to do everything in life. So don't limit yourself while you're still young…there's plenty of other people who are willing to do that for you. You can accomplish anything if you set your mind to it. Realize that major victories are the result of many small efforts.

Work hard every day. Be diligent in your studies. These are two of the things that great accomplishments are made of.

Sometimes you'll succeed and sometimes you'll fail. Don't let this fact slow you down. There is usually a degree of pain associated with going outside your comfort zone. You'll get stuck if you don't accept some risk. I hope you continue to expand your lives in new and exciting directions.

Communicate. So much of our unhappiness arises from our unwillingness to engage in honest dialogue with others. When talking about something is the most difficult, you probably need to do it the most. I will always be here for you when you need to talk. Don't be reluctant to seek out help when you need it. No one said we have to do it all alone.

Be nice to others. Have compassion for their sufferings. Avoid gossip. Your friends' feelings can be hurt just as easily as yours can. On the other hand, speak out against injustice. Do not tolerate abuse.

There are many ways to define a successful life. Ask yourself what you would like people to say about you when you are old. How do you want to feel about yourself? Then let that guide your decisions and actions. Be a person of integrity. Honor your commitments whenever possible—especially your commitments to yourself. But, also learn to forgive yourself. Perfection is a futile goal.

Finally, and perhaps most important:

Make your spiritual development a lifetime journey. Some truths are universal; some might apply to you alone. Seek them out and try to let your actions be guided by them. Find ways and take the time to tap into your Buddha nature—that place where you are filled with wisdom and compassion for yourself and others. Add your own uniqueness to the tapestry of human life. And respect others' uniqueness as they go about their journeys. In this way, you will be able to make the most of each precious moment.

Always know you have a father who loves you more than life itself!

A Father's Role

. . . .

"OH NO," I thought. Ralph from accounting. Skinny with black horn-rimmed glasses. A compulsive talker, Ralph was a human magnet. If you showed the slightest interest in what he was about to say, you were stuck to him like an iron filing to a magnet—sometimes for hours. And forget interrupting. You couldn't slice your words into small enough pieces to get them in edgewise.

So there was Ralph bemoaning the fact that his wife had just delivered their first child and he had no idea what his responsibilities, as a father, should be. I took pity. I mean, after all, as a Buddhist and a father of two, I couldn't just desert him. So I suggested he use his own father as an example. Leaving Ralph with a startled look, I backed out of my office door and practically ran down the narrow hallway.

Just as I pushed the down elevator button, congratulating myself on such a clever escape, a meek voice called out, "But I was an orphan." Wouldn't you know it? An orphan! I promised Ralph I would spend the weekend researching the role of a father in modern society and share amazing insights with him on Monday.

This appeared to satisfy him. Knowing I had to take my commitment seriously, I determined to chant about this. And so my quest began.

My first priority—find my wife. Our many years together had convinced me that if anyone could answer this question with authority, it would be Most Beautiful One—teacher and mother. No problem. Watch out, Ralph.

I found my wife at my younger daughter's soccer game. She was standing in the oppressive heat beneath a swarm of gnats the size of golf balls. Waving my arms furiously (these killer bugs hate soccer fathers), I asked her what single cause I could make to be a better father.

"Simple," she replied as several screaming girls hurled themselves at our daughter on the soccer field. "Stop burping at the dinner table. It's a disgusting habit and it sets a bad example for the girls."

So there you have it. Straight from an authority. Somehow, while I had to admit she was right, I didn't think I had yet plumbed the depths of this issue.

Then, sympathizing with my obvious frustration, she relayed something she had read by Daisaku Ikeda. "Never look down on a child. In relations with boys and girls, treat them as small adults, as very good friends. Respect the personality of a child, and in conversations with him or her, speak as a true friend when you talk of the problems of life." I thought this advice would be very useful to Ralph.

Later that night, as I drank a non-carbonated beverage at the dinner table, I asked my daughters the same question. Their numerous answers can be summarized as follows: "Mom always gets us things we need. Dad should buy us anything else we want." I wisely dropped the subject and hid my wallet.

Maybe, I thought, I should go to a more mature source of wisdom—my mother-in-law. If anyone would have an opinion about what a father's role should be, especially mine, she would.

Her response was actually very helpful. She said parents should expose their children to a variety of life experiences, because this gives them more choices and opens up their future possibilities. I should probably listen to her more often.

Having overdosed on family input, I decided it was time to get some Buddhist input. So, I called Joe, a member of our Buddhist community. He was involved in cooking eggs with his two small children. Our conversation was, of necessity, interrupted with shouts of warning, fear and panic punctuated with squeals of delight. He said he thought a father should feel the responsibility to protect his family. He also said he was once urged to use his Buddhist practice to develop a calm demeanor. Then he would rarely have to scold his children. When a father scolds his child, it is very serious and should only be done when absolutely necessary and with utmost compassion.

While cleaning egg yolk from the floor, Joe added that he had learned that if his attitude and actions were correct and strong enough to make his wife happy, his entire family would be happy. He then quoted a song I have never heard on MTV, "When Mama Ain't Happy, Ain't Nobody Happy." I eagerly assimilated this good advice for Ralph.

Later that afternoon, I played tennis with my friend, Bob. You can't top tennis in 90-percent humidity against a former college all-star for outdoor humiliation. In between beating me in straight sets, Bob said he thought the most difficult challenge for a father was allowing his children to be who they are as opposed to who he thought they should be. We agreed this was very difficult since we have such a strong personal stake in our children's futures.

He said he was struggling to have this attitude with his own son. I shared something I had read by Daisaku Ikeda that one of the important tasks for a father is to use his experience through dialogue with his children to help distill the knowledge they learn in school into living wisdom. This teaches them how to study so that knowledge becomes their flesh and blood. Even if a father travels a lot, someone must fulfill the role of father. So if the father makes up his mind that he will take every chance to have a sensible exchange with his children, then education by the father will have very good results.

I finished my two-hour imitation of wild gnat beating, and Bob helped me limp off the court. After a brief layover at his house for Band-Aids, I returned home to spend some precious time with my daughters. Later I read the following words in the *Living Buddhism* magazine: "What children expect of their father is neither the personification of profound knowledge nor someone with high social status, great fame, a prestigious job or top-flight education. They want a father with a good attitude toward life."

I marveled that in the process of trying to help Ralph, I had discovered several key points about being a father that could improve my relationship with my own children. Considering the benefits we receive when we help others, I probably shouldn't have been so surprised.

Thanks, Ralph.

A Mother's Perspective

. . . .

I T WAS A TYPICAL humid summer evening in 1990, and the eighth floor of our building was extremely quiet at seven o'clock in the evening. That suited me just fine. I was trying to finish a difficult proposal and had the door closed and the answering machine on. The last thing I needed or wanted was a long conversation with Ralph from accounting.

More than two years of Ralph's interruptions should have prepared me for the knock on the balcony outside my office window. What could I do? There stood Ralph in ninety-five-degree weather; hands clenched together pleading with me to talk to him. Some people! Finally I motioned him around and into my office. I guess I felt a little guilty for making him wait outside for five minutes, him sweating and everything.

Nichiren Buddhism describes ten basic conditions of life. These are known as the Ten Worlds and are commonly called hell, hunger, animality, anger, humanity, heaven, learning, realization, bodhisattva and Buddhahood.

At any given moment, we exhibit the characteristics of one of these Ten Worlds. For instance, if someone waves a one hundred-dollar bill (assuming you need money), your senses will experience the condition of hunger. If you are then hit on the top of the head with a newspaper (which would be a very mean thing to do!) your condition of life might change to anger. If the love of your life comforts you, then you will be in the world of heaven. But if the relationship should suddenly end, you might be in the world of hell.

While we all have all Ten Worlds within, we typically experience only the first nine, each one in greater or lesser degrees according to our karma. Buddhist practice exists to help us experience the tenth world of enlightenment or Buddhahood. And, more importantly, to make this state of indestructible happiness, wisdom, compassion and courage our fundamental life tendency. Nichiren revealed a simple and practical method for us to manifest this enlightenment in our everyday lives.

Each time I encountered Ralph, I discovered that the ninth world of bodhisattva, or helping others, doesn't come easily.

"Hi, Ralph. I'm kind of busy right now. What's on your mind?" I anxiously asked.

"Gee, Mike. I'll only take a minute. I've got a real problem at home and figured you might be able to help, you being an experienced father and all."

(Obviously Ralph had figured out how to flatter me to get my attention. Am I that transparent?)

I waved Ralph to a chair, turned off the computer— so much for my proposal deadline—and prepared to practice a good dialogue technique by seeking to understand before being understood.

Ralph continued, "You see, little Ralph Junior has been awfully difficult, and my wife, Mary Jean...well, you know, a lot of responsibilities at home fall on her shoulders and lately she's been real unhappy. I just don't know what to do."

"Hmm," I muttered. Ralph waited expectantly.

"Look, Ralph, we'll probably never be able to completely understand the challenges facing mothers. But I'm sure there's something you can do to improve the situation. Just give me a little time to explore the problem, and I'll get back to you."

Ralph nodded reluctantly and shuffled slowly down the hall. It was the first time he had ever ended a conversation voluntarily. I was determined to come up with something to encourage him by the next morning.

Before I left work that night, I called my friend Nina. We have worked together off and on for more than ten years and she always has some interesting thoughts. I told her I was trying to understand a mother's perspective so I could help a friend. I could hear little Jeffrey and Annie energetically running around in the background.

"You know, Mike, in some ways I think all women, especially mothers, are seeking to discover their own mother."

"Huh?" I interrupted impatiently. "Don't most women already know who that is?"

"Sure they do," she answered. "But by mother I mean

a metaphor for that community of older, wiser women who understand and listen to younger women and who encourage and pass on traditions and life experiences. It's often very lonely and isolated, especially for mothers who stay at home all day with their children."

"Yeah. I remember how desperate for adult conversation Most Beautiful One was when our kids were younger," I said.

"Well, then you can see how important such a community of women is." She paused and added, "There aren't too many places for women to go to find that encouragement. So each of us has to search for sources of nourishment from people and groups around us."

Our Buddhist community provides such an environment, I thought. "So, what do you think I should tell my friend?"

"I think he should really listen to what his wife is saying and provide her with understanding and, most important, his determination to be an equal partner in raising their children."

I thanked Nina, closed up shop and hit the freeway. Next, I called a Buddhist friend, Barbara, from my car. She has an older daughter in California who is an actress.

"Barbara," I asked, "can you help me understand the challenges a mother faces?"

"Hold on a minute," she said. "I'm trying to program the VCR to tape a TV program that's on later today." I settled down for what I figured would be a long wait. If being able to program a VCR was ever made a criterion for enlightenment, I wouldn't stand a chance!

"Okay," Barbara said. She was taping an episode of *Santa Barbara* that her daughter was appearing in. "Now, what did you want to know?"

I explained Ralph's situation, without using his name. She said the biggest challenge for her, especially having been a single parent for several years before remarrying, had been to avoid getting carried away and yelling at her daughter. She had learned that it was important to keep her perspective.

"Also," she added, "have you ever noticed mothers are not allowed to be sick or tired?"

"Yes," I had to admit. "If everyone else is too tired or too sick or just doesn't want to do a chore, they know that good ol' mom will be there."

"It's not very fair," she remarked.

"No," I agreed, "it sure isn't." At that moment, I turned into our neighborhood, passed through a cell phone black hole and lost the connection. Modern technology still has a long way to go.

I parked in the garage and, as I threw a load of laundry in the dryer, heard yelling from upstairs. It seemed our dog, a sheltie, was nowhere to be found. Finally we discovered her in my twelve-year-old daughter Jamie's room under a pile of laundry. Left to her own devices, Jamie could easily live for six months without putting away her clothes. This upsets her mother to no end.

After work Most Beautiful One sought input from her friend Becky. She stressed the importance of each member of the family respecting each other. Becky had said, "You're not doing children a favor by picking up after them and not giving them any responsibility. Even if they're unconcerned about their messes, it affects the rest of the family and that should concern them."

"On the other hand," she continued, "the mother needs to avoid being the family nag. She should appreciate the positive characteristics her children have instead of focusing on what they aren't doing. There's a sense of balance between appreciation and helping them gain a sense of responsibility. The challenge is to use our Buddhist practice to have sufficient wisdom and hope to be able to reach children in a manner that will motivate them."

Most Beautiful One had also heard that we get the best response when we address a person's Buddha nature, politely and calmly carrying out dialogue and sometimes, depending on the situation, mercifully correcting that person. In the course of such human interaction, the enlightened nature in that person, reflecting our own sincerity, will respond to us in return.

We reflected on how this advice applied to our relationship with our children and agreed that all the wonderful qualities of both our daughters, by far, outweighed their few bad habits. Just minutes later, I tripped over their pajamas, which littered our bathroom. Oh well, I thought, Rome wasn't built in a day.

I felt almost ready to talk to Ralph. But I decided to make one last call to another good friend, Sandra. Sandra had raised five children and was one of the most giving people I have ever met. When I called, she was "experiencing" her thirteen-year-old son, Gary, after a several-hour electricity blackout and NO NINTENDO! I think she welcomed my phone call. Actually, I think at that point even a firing squad would have been welcome. Anyway, she told me her desire as a mother was to develop the patience and wisdom to deal with children on all levels. She said she believed her capacity as a human being increased each day because she learned so much from her children.

"Instead of wondering what's wrong with them," she said, "I ask myself why I can't understand their situation. I'm the one who must change."

As usual, in trying to find an answer to one of Ralph's problems, I had gathered additional ammunition in my quest to improve my own life. I was determined, as a father and husband, to try even harder to give my wife and children a supportive and warm environment so that they could display their full capabilities. And the best place to start, I thought—as I went upstairs to chant—was to go upstairs to chant!

Mating for Life

. . . .

M Y WIFE AND I took a glass-bottom boat trip during our summer 2000 vacation to British
Columbia. We were staying for ten days in a bed and
breakfast on the beach in Tofino, a small resort on the
west coast of Vancouver Island. Famous for the sever-
ity of its winter storms, it also has a cool summer climate that is ideal for someone who suffers from MS
symptoms.

The Tofino locals joked about the "glass-bottom"
boat...it was actually just a long slice of glass embed-
ded in a narrow wooden box in the bottom of the boat
and, if you looked really carefully, you could see some
water and sea kelp floating by.

The boat's captain, John, was a kind, older man with
skin weathered by years in the sun. In a patient voice, he
explained that the village on an island we were floating
by was more than ten thousand years old. It was where
he lived with his small son, who helped him on the boat.
It was the oldest continuously inhabited village on the
entire west coast. Pretty impressive. I couldn't help wondering if my own hometown in Virginia would still be
inhabited in ten thousand years. And, if so, what would

it be like? Would there still be a Starbucks? McDonalds? Soccer league sign-ups? Trees?

On the way, John stopped near a small island so that we could appreciate the two resident eagles and their large nest. There is about one nest per acre in British Columbia, an extremely high density as eagles go. These two had returned to the same nest for the last seven years and this year had two baby eagles. Usually, only the strongest young eagle survives but both of these had made it. While we watched in awe, the mother eagle spread her wings and took a brief flight over the inlet. We could see her white head and the powerful beating of her wings. John explained that eagles mate for life and that one of them always stays close by the young eagles until they are old enough to take off on their own.

Mate for life. I held Trude's thin hand tightly when I heard that. If I had to describe my relationship with my wife in just three words, it would be this—mate for life. Not everyone is like an eagle. Some people must be meant to be more solitary creatures like the gray whale that is perfectly happy feeding in a group or by itself.

When I first spied Trude at a high school dance in 1967, I wasn't thinking about mating for life. I was more fixated on her attractive cheerleader legs and bright smile. Still, it wasn't but a few dates later that I began to fall madly, almost obsessively, in love with her.

An eagle must first learn how to fly and hunt under the watchful eyes of its parents before it takes off on its own to eventually find a mate and begin the job of nest building and raising children. My parents weren't very watchful, and I lacked some of the basic survival skills necessary to excel in our modern society. My parents meant well, but were ill-equipped to help me. I don't think it unfair to say that Trude not only became my sweetheart but also provided me with the emotional stability I needed at that time.

Together, we discovered the mysteries of poetry, long walks and camping and somehow managed to embark together on a lifetime journey of self-discovery. Much of our path revolved around our relationship— we were perfect mirrors for each other—and our Buddhist practice.

It must be nice to be an eagle. By your very nature, you live in the moment without the daily distractions of your mind whispering self-deflating thoughts. You know what you're supposed to do and with whom and you never question why. I can see now that what I have so desperately sought my whole life is the simplicity of the eagle: to know who I am or, more correctly, to accept myself as I am with all my strengths and weaknesses.

In a letter to one of his followers, Niike, Nichiren wrote, "A bird's egg contains nothing but liquid, yet by itself this develops into a beak, two eyes, and all the other parts, and the bird soars into the sky. We, too, are the eggs of ignorance, which are pitiful things, but when nurtured by the chanting of Nam-myoho-renge-kyo, which is like the warmth of the mother bird, we develop the beak of the thirty-two features and the feathers of the eighty characteristics and are free to soar into the sky of the true aspect of all phenomena and the reality of all things."

So I continue to develop my awareness that I am unconditionally a Buddha as I am, not only if I change this or that or accomplish this or that. A baby eagle is born with this awareness. I, on the other hand, have spent a lifetime learning that I am already who and where I need to be.

Ashby, the Wonder Dog

I would never dare disparage you, for you are all certain to attain Buddhahood.

—FROM *The Lotus Sutra*

FOR SEVERAL YEARS, if you came to a Buddhist discussion meeting at our house, you would park in a cul de sac surrounded by numerous tall, leafy trees in suburban Virginia, outside of Washington, D.C. Trudging up our driveway in the humidity or the snow, you would approach a two-story colonial home. A note on the front door would tell you to enter, saying something like: "The happiest people in the world meet here. Come on in." You would immediately be greeted by a very small tri-color sheltie. No ordinary animal, this would be Ashby Never Disparaging, the Wonder Dog! Like Bodhisattva Never Disparaging (a bodhisattva described in the Lotus Sutra who expressed respect to everyone regardless of how they treated him), she dealt with everyone with the utmost reverence.

We had Ashby for almost ten years. Early one evening in 1999, I guess her little body just got too tired and she died like we all will someday. We're still feeling waves of sadness, wonder and appreciation for her presence in our lives.

In our busy society, it's easy to take important things for granted until we need them or, like Ashby, they are physically no longer with us. This reminds me of how interconnected my life is to my surroundings and to the lives of others, even animals. While scooting around on four stubby legs, Ashby taught me some extremely valuable lessons about how to cherish each and every moment.

> *No act of kindness, no matter how small, is ever wasted.*
> —AESOP, FROM *The Lion and the Mouse*

Ashby was an equal opportunity pooch. She had a way of opening up her life to every single person she came in contact with. At our monthly community center world peace prayer meeting, several people reminisced how Ashby would go from person to person during the meetings in our home pushing up against them until they scratched her. I can't count the times she caused us all to laugh as she rolled over on to her back during particularly intense discussions.

Ashby had one lifetime enemy—the evil vacuum cleaner. Her weekly mission was to defeat this device by barking nonstop for two hours and spinning in circles until the cleaning was done. I think she actually believed her vigorous behavior caused that particular instrument to be exiled to the hall closet. Goethe, the philosopher, wrote, "It is better to do the smallest thing in the world than to hold half an hour to be too small a thing." Ashby really put her whole life into whatever she was doing.

Life is filled with potholes. That's just the way it is. I think we humans, having more complex minds than canines, are compelled to create more obstacles for ourselves. Earlier this year, Trude and I were trying to decide whether to move back to the milder California climate for her health or stay in Virginia. It was a very challenging and emotional change to consider—something we would both have to be happy with for it to work. A friend from Los Angeles pointed out that any decision we made would present us with continued challenges to overcome. And that it wasn't so much what we decided to do that mattered, as how we went about doing it.

Then, an unexpected thing happened. While we prayed to be able to move at the right time and in the right way, and while we talked and changed our mind every five minutes, we began to realize how connected we were to our many friends in Virginia. We also took an objective look at the many stresses involved in reestablishing ourselves somewhere new and the negative effect that might have on Trude's health.

It's hard to describe the deep appreciation we felt when we decided to remain in Virginia. A few weeks later, I ended up losing an executive marketing position that I no longer had any passion for and was able to successfully start my own consulting company. In 2004, after five years of my being self-employed, we had the confidence and financial independence to move to the Seattle area.

I've now replaced the perception of security at my old job with a deeper security—a confidence in my Buddhist practice and in my own capabilities. Dogs don't seem to worry about this stuff. They pretty much take each day as it comes. I suspect they have an easier mind to master.

> *Unless we live fully right now, not sometime in the future, true fulfillment in life will forever elude us. Rather than putting things off till the future, we should find meaning in life, thinking and doing what is most important right now, right where we are—setting our hearts aflame and igniting our lives. Otherwise, we cannot lead an inspired existence.*
> —DAISAKU IKEDA

I don't think Ashby would mind me revealing that she wasn't the smartest creature in the animal kingdom. Even after ten years, she still wasn't quite sure the dog door in our family room would let her outside. And when we called her name, she would often run in the wrong direction. But I once read about one of Shakyamuni Buddha's disciples, Chudapanthaka, who had gained enlightenment although (or maybe because) he was not very bright. However, he had an incredible seeking mind. It took him many years to remember a one-sentence phrase. So maybe that explains why Ashby had such an enlightened effect on everyone.

I've learned through my Buddhist practice that I've been a Buddha all along and so I can choose my own reality. It is this realization that is enabling me more than ever to experience joy no matter what is happening around me. Even when I'm experiencing a profound loss.

Ashby stopped breathing at exactly the same moment I sat down to chant for her suffering to end. When the doctor took X-rays, he called to say he had never seen such a large heart in an animal her size. I could have told him that.

Dialogue and Diversity

Imagine Peace

I wrote this essay after attending an inspiring women's peace conference co-sponsored by the SGI-USA at the World Bank in February 2001.

S OMETIMES I need to remove the punctuation from my life the barriers of understanding that separate me from other people and other ways of looking at the world

Sometimes it is not easy to break out of the masculine side of my experience of my genetic code that would have me withdraw from the connectedness that is so vital to a better world

Withdraw behind the walls of a security that is not really security at all

There are times when I am moved to tears by the willingness of women to fight for peace to engage for peace to build for peace for all our children

I spent the day at the World Bank in Washington DC with twenty-five hundred women who dare to imagine peace not just for themselves but for the entire world

Women of every size and shape and color and temperament and desire and talent and age

Women rich and poor and lonely and alone and wife and partner and mother and professional

I spent today with thousands of angels of peace me an alien from another planet fortunate to be in their presence awed by their commitment inspired by their vision

Sometimes I must break down the punctuation in my life that would prevent me from seeing to the other side

Put aside the commas and the periods and the exclamation marks so that perhaps I can see some truth

Like the truth of chorus men who diligently and individually rehearsed their music their task while a chorus woman decided out loud that she would dedicate her song to her husband and children who could not be there

And in these two simple but profound punctuated differences of how we men and you women approach the moment I choose to see real hope for us together because it is this balance that we so desperately must find

I hear the truth that this must be the century when women come into full partnership and I realize this is the same path I have traveled with my mate for more than thirty years

Mine must not be yet another marriage or this another century of masculine dominance but one of equal partnership

I spent today with the spirit of three billion women many who will never know the blessings of freedom

Who continue to be systematically punctuated out of

existence by uncaring male dominated religious and political systems

Can you hear their angry cries Afghanistan the women of the world cry out to you

I heard their cries this morning and my heart broke and I could barely contain my grief

Or my joy as I remembered the many women in my life who for fifty years convinced me I was worthy of love long before I learned to love myself

These women who I would name but for a lack of space

I talked to my daughters today as women not children as keepers of the future confident that they would face their challenges with compassion how could a father ask for more

And my wife who continues to amaze me in every way who has the courage to understand both my male and female sides and the patience for me to learn which to use

Sometimes I need to remove the punctuation from my life so that I can remember to respect and listen to the women around me

The world is a much more wonderful place with them at my side

Getting to Know You

....

Dinner at Bea's — Part One

Part one of Dinner at Bea's was originally written in 1993 as a modern thesis on one of the major writings of Nichiren, "On Establishing the Correct Teaching for the Peace of the Land." Nichiren wrote this letter in the form of questions and answers between a host and a guest.

THE SPINDLY LOOKING MAN shook the rain off his gray overcoat as the door to the old diner clanged shut behind him. The train-car-style restaurant was almost empty; a Suzanne Vega recording played softly in the background. He sat down opposite a young woman with a disheveled appearance — more in her demeanor than in her choice of clothes.

Sweeping aside the pepper and salt shakers, he said, "Sorry I'm late...the rain, wouldn't you know."

She looked up at him curiously. "I'm not sure why I'm here. I mean, what with the troubles all over the world, I feel a little ridiculous wasting your time discussing my problems."

The man smiled warmly but said nothing in response.

She fidgeted nervously with a plastic fork, picking at the white tongs. "I've always wanted to help society, you know. Ever since I was a teenager. Save the whales...ban the bomb...help the battered. That was me. But now I'm in my thirties and those goals have faded, or rather, I should say, have been replaced with an emptiness." She paused for a moment, then added, "My sister says you can tell me how to change this. You know, I've been a supporter of the SGI for several years, but frankly I don't see how anything you can say will explain why the world is in such sorry shape."

The man encouraged her to go on, asking, "What do you think is the cause of these troubles?"

"Well," she replied, "I'm not really sure. I guess most of the problems I see, like hunger and war, are caused by evil or incompetent leaders and corrupt governments."

"Hmm," he muttered. "As you know from your sister, I also practice Nichiren Daishonin's Buddhism. More than seven hundred years ago, Nichiren dealt with the same questions we are discussing today. And because of the universality of Nam-myoho-renge-kyo, his responses are as valid today as they were in that ancient age."

"But," she interrupted, "I know something about the history of the Far East, and the disturbances back then were completely different from those we face today."

"Were they?" he asked. "In a letter to the acting regent of Japan titled 'On Establishing the Correct Teaching for the Peace of the Land,' Nichiren described three calamities and seven disasters. The disasters included invasion, internal strife, untimely storms and deaths from epidemics. These sound very much like the ills of our society today, such as the world food shortage, AIDS, environmental destruction and the population explosion."

"By the way," he continued, "Many of the disasters Nichiren described had already befallen the Japanese people because of their devotion to dehumanizing philosophies. Only two of the seven hadn't occurred: invasion and internal strife. Nichiren, out of his deep compassion and at the risk of his very life, spoke out and warned the government that unless it abandoned misguided philosophies soon, these two disasters would occur."

"Are you telling me that a person's or nation's life philosophy can affect the weather or the health of a people? You are kidding, aren't you?"

"Absolutely not," he assured her. "Back then, just as in our present society, leaders found it convenient to blame these strange and terrible occurrences on chance or on the inherent evil in humankind.

"However, Nichiren revealed the true cause of human suffering: negative effects that arise from an adherence to philosophies that ignore the dignity of human life. And, sure enough, when the regent of Japan ignored his warning, the invasions and internal strife predicted by Nichiren occurred, further proving the validity of his teachings."

"You know, this is all very interesting. But I really don't see the relevance," she complained.

"Well, before we're done talking tonight, I hope I can convince you that not only are the problems facing the world today the same as those in Nichiren's time, but that the three calamities and seven disasters mirror the unhappiness and lack of good fortune in our lives."

At just that moment, the café's proprietress, an older, platinum blonde with a probable taste for too many hot apple pies, came over to take their order. Her nametag introduced her as Beatrice. A steady trail of raindrops continued to paint the diner windows.

> *Teach others to the best of your ability, even if it*
> *is only a single sentence or phrase.*
> —NICHIREN

They took the time to share a little of their background while they ate overcooked hamburgers and greasy fries. He discussed his humble beginnings and increased happiness that had come into his life. She spoke, rather tenuously at first, of forgotten dreams, lost loves and the lonely anguish she was now experiencing.

He was somewhat surprised to discover she was a very successful advertising executive. She, in turn, was intrigued by his position as a professor at the university and even more so at his having been a Buddhist for more than fifteen years. As Bea cleared the table and left a carafe of coffee, they returned to their initial conversation.

"Let's go back to your original frustration," he said. "You name a problem in the world today, and let's see if we can understand it in light of Buddhism."

"Okay. How about the prevalence of substance abuse in our society. Why, it's so pervasive; even my boss takes drugs."

The man thought for a moment. "The president of our Buddhist organization, Daisaku Ikeda, has said that when your life truly changes, the sound and impact of your voice will also change. Have you noticed how taking drugs drains people's life-energy?"

"Of course. Medical science has shown that to be true."

"Yes, I suppose so. But what science hasn't been able to clearly quantify yet is that substance abuse is a reflection of an inherent lack of happiness, an inability on the part of an individual to control his or her own destiny. As a result, people hide behind drugs or alcohol, and their erroneous thoughts drain their life force. So while drug programs provide some relief in the near term, only by freeing addicts from their dependency on drugs with a positive influence, like Buddhism, can we truly eliminate this terrible problem."

"Okay," she said. "Devastating storms like Hurricane Andrew...I suppose you're going to tell me it was because of the inherent evil of the Florida lottery!"

The man's eyebrows raised slightly as he laughed. "No, I think the cause is much more deeply rooted within our lives. You have to realize that the law of cause and effect is very strict. Just because we don't want to believe that we are responsible for the effects in our environment doesn't mean it isn't so. Even though we may not have the wisdom to identify exactly which causes we have made to suffer a natural disaster, we can begin to make the right causes to eliminate misfortune from our lives.

"A more contemporary example is Germany during World War II," he continued.

"My parents came to the United States to escape the persecution," she interjected.

"That must have been a frightening experience for them," he responded. "I'm sure you'd agree that the German people mistakenly embraced a tremendously destructive philosophy. Last year, I was at a seminar in Amsterdam. One evening, as the sun was setting, I took a boat ride along several of the city's canals. We docked at the house where young Anne Frank lived while she hid from the German soldiers. Seeing that house really brought home to me how destructive, how incredibly senseless war is, and how it is truly the innocent and the young who suffer the most. It makes me appreciate the SGI and other peace organizations' strong condemnation of armed conflict as a solution to the world's problems.

"Anyway, the history books are filled with terrible effects of the misuse of religion for evil purposes. Nichiren Buddhism, on the other hand, has spread in a very peaceful manner, able to coexist with other religions."

"I'm still not convinced."

The man paused for a moment, pouring them each some more coffee while collecting his thoughts.

"People today refuse to take responsibility for their misfortunes. The technical mistakes that result in airline accidents or oil spills are rarely admitted. Neither are our own roles in failed marriages or careers. But ignorance of the law of cause and effect does not excuse us from suffering the consequences of following an incorrect philosophy any more than it is a valid excuse for forgetting to pay our taxes."

The young woman, who had seemed more relaxed, now became so agitated that she tipped over her coffee cup. He quickly wiped up the mess, which she ignored.

"Do you mean to imply," she demanded, "that I am responsible for all the problems around me? Why that's the most ridiculous thing I've ever heard. No wonder my sister no longer dates you!"

Saying this, she excused herself and marched off to the restroom, leaving the man to chant under his breath, pondering how fortunate he was to have encountered a philosophy that allowed him to accept responsibility for his own life and how difficult it was for others to embrace that sometimes harsh reality. Still, he thought, I can't give up. Somehow I must find a way to give this woman hope!

> *If they do not shake off these delusions that they cling to but continue to harbor erroneous views,*

*then they will quickly leave this world of the living
and surely fall into the hell of incessant suffering.*
—NICHIREN

The diner had only one small restroom. The white enamel had chipped off the metal partitions and there were long cracks in the dull mirror. The young woman angrily ran a brush through her long, tangled hair. The recognition that she had lost control of her emotions did little to assuage her anger. Seeing her pathetic image in a slice of the broken mirror, she sat sullenly on the toilet seat lid. Blue mascara flowed down her flushed cheeks.

"Damn him!" she cried out loud.

It was as if he were seeing right into her soul. It was unnerving. She doubted he knew the details of her recent divorce or her dissatisfaction with the ethical dilemmas caused by her profession. No, she realized, his insight came from somewhere else…somewhere much deeper.

But the nerves he touched were still much too raw, too exposed. She had promised herself that no one would ever do that to her again. Still, if only there were a way, a light, some kind of hope. But no, not for her, not tonight. She determined to straighten herself up, try to salvage some of her dignity and escape to the safety of her own apartment.

She avoided his eyes as she walked back into the eating area. Instead of sitting down, she reached across the seat to fetch her overcoat from the corner of the booth.

"I don't believe we have anything else to talk about," she said.

He squirmed slightly in his seat but managed to calmly reply, "Please let me explain myself."

He waved her into her seat. Something inside told him that she really did want his help but was just too proud to admit it.

"A basic premise underlying this letter of Nichiren's is the oneness of life and its environment. You might say it mirrors 'the good news-bad news' saying. The bad news is that at some time in the past, we have each made the causes for whatever situation we find ourselves in— our good fortune, or lack of it, our family, our health and so on. However, the good news is that we have within our lives the power to change our surroundings for the better."

"Can you run that by me again?" she asked as she haltingly took her seat.

"Sure." He picked up a white napkin and sketched a small diagram of a person's body and a shadow. "Let's say this person represents your life, and the shadow it casts on the wall, your surroundings—your job, your friends, your finances. Notice what happens to the shadow when the body is bent."

The owner shook her head to herself as she walked by. "Another late night," she thought.

"It bends also. So what?" the young woman replied.

"Well, if our environment is a mess, then our life must be too," he said.

"But," she said, her earlier defenses resurfacing, "what about other people who mess with your life? How do you explain that?"

He could tell from the expectant look on her face that their discussion was rapidly approaching a very sensitive subject. How could he relate the basic premise of Nichiren's letter without upsetting her, he wondered. He took a deep breath (actually quite a few very deep breaths) and continued.

"You know, for several years I was convinced my troubles were caused by my parents, my employer, and, when no one else was available to blame, by society in general. Later, through this practice, I came to realize that I was just relying on others for my happiness, and that I would remain unhappy until I took responsibility for my own life. Of course, this didn't excuse the negative behavior of others, but ultimately it was me who had to change.

"Nichiren points this out very clearly. And even though this law of cause and effect is very strict, by accepting the reality of the example of the body and its shadow, and by chanting Nam-myoho-renge-kyo, we make the changes necessary to transform our unfortunate situations to fortunate ones."

Will the future ever arrive?...Should we continue to look upwards?...The ideal is terrifying to

behold, lost as it is in the depths...threatened on all
sides by the dark forces that surround it; neverthe-
less, no more in danger than a star in the jaws of
the clouds.

—Victor Hugo from *Les Misérables*

Several more examples and quite a few crumpled nap-
kins later, she finally asked, "What does this have to do
with creating world peace? I mean, I'm only one person
out of billions."

"Yes, but Nichiren explained that a country is com-
posed of individuals, and that world peace will be
achieved when enough of these people change their destiny through chanting Nam-myoho-renge-kyo.

"So rather than passing another law or regulation or
fighting another war to end all wars, Nichiren Buddhists
are engaged in the most significant daily struggle of all:
challenging the devilish conditions within their own
lives and sharing the resulting joy with others in their
families, workplaces and elsewhere in society."

"But isn't that a cop-out? I mean, what about the need
for revolution to change society? Why, we wouldn't even
have the United States if it weren't for a revolution."

"Good point," he commented. "I saw the musical *Les
Misérables* recently. Are you familiar with the story?"

"Sure. I saw it last year in New York."

"Well, it's interesting to note that while the workers
were successful in overthrowing the king, with the resulting rise of the bourgeoisie, it was actually the middle

class that benefited in the long run. This is just another example of one mistaken philosophy being replaced by another. This is often the case with revolutions. Daisaku Ikeda says what we need is a true human revolution based on the dignity of human life and the concept of the oneness of life and the environment. This means that each of us does make a difference."

"Hmm…This oneness of life and environment business makes a lot of sense. And I can see from your explanation that the various ills suffered by society today could actually be caused by our adherence to incorrect views. I'll really have to think about what you've said." She tilted her head sideways and, with a teasing smile, added, "Where were you ten years ago! If only I'd listened to my sister and started this practice back then."

The man quickly reached across the linoleum table and grasped her hands in his. "No reason to have regrets. Rather, with the spirit of 'from this moment onward,' why not begin practicing this great philosophy and prove the power of Nam-myoho-renge-kyo to yourself? I'm confident that you will then finally realize your childhood dream of making a concrete contribution to the realization of a more peaceful world."

Glancing over to the counter, he noticed Beatrice looking nervously at her watch. He quietly helped the young woman with her coat. They waited outside in a light drizzle for a taxi, each lost in thought—she at her good fortune to have met this strange man; he with a deep appreciation for Nichiren and the incredibly timeless insight of "On Establishing the Correct Teaching for the Peace of the Land."

They stood together under the blue neon sign, its flickering letters proudly announcing, "Bea's Diner— saving the world one bite at a time."

The Benefit of the Doubt

Dinner at Bea's — Part Two

*Benefits should be distributed a bit at a time
in order that they may be savoured fully.*
—NICCOLO MACHIAVELLI FROM *The Prince*

THE STREET OUTSIDE the diner was buried in more than a foot of snow. A couple in their late thirties sat together in the last booth just as they had every Friday night for the past three months. Bea, the elderly owner, server and cashier, smiled to herself as she washed some spilled coffee off the yellowed Formica counter. A battered wife in her youth, Bea was unusually protective of other women. But even she had to admit that the man, Paul, seemed to have a much needed positive effect on the young lady.

Bea thought her name was Kate. Funny, she referred to most women as "gals." For some reason, Kate was a *lady*. Must be the way she dresses, she mused. Watching them through the wall mirrors behind the old soda fountain, she wondered what they found to talk about for hours on end. She occasionally listened in on their conversations.

There were five booths along a picture window. An

old string of faded colored Christmas lights twinkled across the top. "Gonna have to take those down," Bea thought.

Paul and Kate were sitting in the farthest booth from the door. There were also eight empty swivel stools covered in yellow plastic at the counter across from the booths. Frank, the white-haired cook and dishwasher, could be seen through an opening in the wall as he grilled hamburgers for the two customers. The patties barely resembled meat but the regulars loved them. Frank Sinatra, no relation to the cook, sang softly from one of the tiny juke boxes, a selection from a previous customer.

Bea remembered the first night Paul and Kate had met. She hadn't really expected to see them together again. Their first encounter had been tumultuous to say the least...intense talking by Paul punctuated with fits of yelling and a tearful visit to the bathroom by Kate. But they returned a week later and appeared, from the fact they were sitting on the same side of the table, to have made significant progress in their relationship.

The streetlights outside flickered behind the falling snow.

> *There is a Scottish saying that if you remain silent, it will be to your disadvantage. It is far more enjoyable and beneficial to open-heartedly develop dialogue with others than to maintain a lonely silence.*
> —DAISAKU IKEDA

"I don't understand why you don't call Susan. Not talking isn't going to solve anything."

Paul loved the way Kate waved her hands around when she spoke. "I've tried, Kate. Honest. She doesn't want to hear from me. We only just got close in the last few years."

"Well," Kate replied, "I suppose I can't blame her. After all, you did insult her boyfriend and her doctor in the same evening."

"Gee, thanks for the support." Paul fidgeted with the straw in his diet Coke.

"Sorry, I didn't mean that...I mean what I meant was..."

"To be mean, that's what you meant!"

Paul looked forlorn. Kate looked amused. Bea looked away.

"You know, Paul," Kate said, "this is the first time since we met that I've actually seen you look discouraged. What happened...lose your favorite set of prayer beads?" Although Kate had started chanting, her practice was tenuous and she enjoyed teasing Paul over the intensity of his faith.

"Problems are a part of the practice," Paul replied somewhat defensively.

"I prefer the benefits."

"Well, so do I. But my biggest benefits always seem to follow major obstacles. Believe me, if I could just pass go and collect my two hundred dollars without the suffering, I would!"

"And how," muttered Bea from behind the counter. Both Paul and Kate looked over at her, but she busied herself placing pickles and potato chips on their platters before bringing them to their table. They ate their meal in silence for a while. Wiping some ketchup from her mouth with her napkin, Kate reached into her large cloth purse and withdrew a newspaper clipping.

"Uh, oh," Paul cried. "Last time you did this we argued for more than two hours. Maybe I'd better order another dinner. I might need the energy." He laughed. She grimaced.

"Look," she said. "You told me to study and so I just thought you might want to hear this. If you'd rather not..."

"I'm sorry," Paul said apologetically. "Please, go ahead. I was just kidding."

Kate put on her reading glasses (he thought they made her eyes look even more beautiful).

She read, "Whether we regard difficulties in life as misfortunes or whether we view them as good fortune depends entirely on how much we have forged our inner determination. It all depends on our attitude, our inner state of life."

He encouraged her to continue reading.

"With a dauntless spirit, we can lead a cheerful and thoroughly enjoyable life. We can develop a 'self' of such fortitude that we look forward to life's trials and tribulations with a sense of profound elation and joy."

I thought it might be encouraging to you since you

seem to be struggling with accepting your sister's illness."

"Yeah. You know, I think I'm mostly just mad at myself for chewing out her boyfriend . . . ."

"Well, he is her doctor."

"Yeah, I know. But he's so arrogant. Like anyone really knows how to treat cancer."

Kate reached over and squeezed Paul's hand. She liked the way he kept his nails neatly trimmed. Matter of fact, she like a lot of things about him.

She noticed his tears but didn't comment. After awhile, he leaned over and kissed her lightly on the cheek.

"It just doesn't seem fair," she commented. "Susan's illness. I mean, she's one of the nicest people I know."

Paul nodded his head. Then he said, "I've thought a lot about things since she got sick."

"What kind of things?"

"You know, life and death, karma, benefits, religion …whether the Orioles will ever have another winning season."

Kate laughed. "No, seriously. I want to know what you've been thinking."

"Oh, I was just thinking about that song you like so much by the Vertigo Girls."

"Uh, Paul," she interrupted. "That's Indigo, not Vertigo."

"Really?" he asked.

"Absolutely. I listen to it sometimes when I'm waiting for you." She inserted a quarter from her purse into the jukebox on their table and selected the song called "Galileo."

> *And now I'm serving time for mistakes made by*
> *another in another lifetime how long till my soul*
> *gets it right can any human being ever reach that*
> *kind of light, I call on the resting soul of galileo*
> *king of night vision, king of insight.*
> —INDIGO GIRLS FROM THE SONG "Galileo"

They nursed their coffee while listening to the music. It had very moving lyrics about reincarnation and paying off karmic debt from past lifetimes. When the song ended, Kate said, "Paul, I've been chanting for three months. And while I have to admit to feeling happier than I've ever felt before, there are still so many things in my life I want to change. You've been practicing for more than fifteen years and you still have problems, too. I don't understand why I'm not getting all the benefits I want now if this practice really works."

"You mean," Paul added in a singing voice, "how long till your soul gets it right?"

"Yeah, I guess so," she said.

"That's what's amazing about this philosophy. It really does allow you to lessen your negative karma and to create good fortune in your life." Paul paused for Kate to consider what he had just said.

Inconspicuous benefit: Benefit that accumulates over a period of time and is not immediately recognizable.
—FROM *The Soka Gakkai Dictionary of Buddhism*

Finally, she responded, "Lots of religions promise a better life in the future."

"Sure," he said, "and there are numerous self-help practices that result in near-term conspicuous benefits. Why, many people achieve great material goals just through hard work. But the real test of a religion is its ability to provide meaningful inconspicuous benefits over a long period of time—in this lifetime—not just after we die. And I would maintain that the most meaningful benefit I can have in my life is the satisfaction that, yes, I am progressing as a human being. That I have the courage and the wisdom to help others and myself when we are in difficult situations."

"And you think chanting does this?" she asked.

"I sure do. Nam-myoho-renge-kyo changes you at a very fundamental level, in a way that influences every aspect of your life...both body and mind."

"And soul?"

"I suspect so," he answered.

Kate thought about this for a moment and then declared, "Aren't you just making excuses for when good things don't happen?"

"It might look that way," Paul answered. "Still, we have to take responsibility for our own past causes...our own karma. I mean, I spent who knows how many life-times making just the right causes to become the con-fused person sitting before you today."

"You can say that again," she said.

"I'd rather not! Seriously, it's human nature to want everything now. I sure do. But the conspicuous benefits we so strongly desire, like better jobs, relationships and money give us the motivation to continue doing our human revolution while even more meaningful changes appear within our lives."

"Such as?" she asked.

"Well," Paul paused for a moment, "take relation-ships. The fact that an incredibly beautiful and intelli-gent woman like you has continued to eat dinner with me for over three months proves that I must have changed something in my life. My previous affairs . . ."

"I beg your pardon," she interrupted indignantly.

"Sorry...poor choice of words. My previous relation-ships have been remarkably short and notable only for their lack of commitment. My sister claims I over-analyze every person I meet. But I've changed dramati-cally in other areas as well...my work habits, energy level and my ability to concentrate on matters at hand instead of always getting distracted. Just the fact I get up in the morning and look forward to the day. I even have reasonable conversations with my father."

Kate shook her head. "Lots of people have reason-able conversations with their parents, Paul, and they don't chant."

Paul nodded. "Hmm. I see your point. But it's like

seeing someone who's an expert at something…a musician, for instance. It seems so effortless. We don't see the years of struggle, the countless times they may have almost given up and so it's difficult for us to understand how much they might have changed. Believe me when I tell you my life is radically different and happier than before I embraced this philosophy."

"That's what your sister said."

Kate went on, "So what you're saying is that 'my soul can get it right this lifetime' through this practice…that it's the inconspicuous changes that occur over a long period of time that are the real lasting benefit?"

"Yeah," he replied, looking somewhat relieved.

In a teasing voice, Kate stated, "Why didn't you just say so?"

> *Benefit of the doubt: a favorable judgment granted in the absence of full evidence.*
> —FROM *The American Heritage Dictionary of the English Language, Fourth Edition*

"You know, Paul," she said, "I really can't say I completely believe in this yet."

"Me either," said Bea as she took a seat in the booth with Kate and Paul. "Mind if I join you? Have to wear earplugs not to hear most of what you're saying," she added as she poured herself a cup of coffee.

"That's okay," he muttered, "I'm perfectly happy to give you both the benefit of the doubt."

"Listen, sweetie," Bea said to Paul, "can't say I really

understand everything you two yap about on Friday nights and I don't mean to be nosy but maybe you should use that practice of yours to get the courage to call your sister...her being sick and all...and would either of you like a slice of warm apple pie?"

In unison, Paul and Kate nodded their heads, grinned and asked, "With vanilla ice cream?"

Life Goes On

. . . .

Dinner at Bea's — Part Three

It took almost seven years to write Part Three of Dinner at Bea's. It started out as an attempt to better grasp the meaning of life and death as a result of losing my older sister to cancer. It wasn't until after the tragic events of September 11, 2001, that I was able to finish it.

> *Ob-la-di, Ob-la-da—life goes on . . .*
> —THE BEATLES FROM THE SONG "Ob-La-Di, Ob-La-Da"

A BURLY ORDERLY was just leaving Paul's sister's room. The first spring sunlight was inching its way through yellowed hospital windowpanes. Paul dodged the orderly and went over to a cracked plastic chair next to a stainless steel service table. On top, untouched oatmeal indicated a lack of appetite typical of chemotherapy treatment patients. The little straw was still stuck to the plastic juice container. Paul wasn't surprised...he couldn't separate them either. He wondered if anyone actually got to drink the juice. Idle thoughts.

As Paul bent over to kiss Susan on the forehead, her eyes opened and she smiled.

"Figured you'd have to visit eventually," she whispered. Her voice cracked from dryness.

Paul didn't answer but handed her a small bottle of water. He collected his thoughts while she sipped.

"Kate seems to think I was close-minded and that I should apologize for the way I treated Rob," he offered.

"Then maybe Kate should have visited instead of you." Her gaze felt like a burning arrow.

Paul was embarrassed. He wondered if coming might have been a mistake. Still, he was here so he might as well try to make things better.

"Look, Sis," he continued, "I'm really sorry. I didn't mean to come off so rude. It's just your illness and feeling so helpless . . ."

"You mean compared to my boyfriend, the mighty doctor?" she interrupted.

"Well, yeah. He acts like he knows all the answers. But look at you…if he's so smart why aren't you getting better?" As soon as the words left his mouth, Paul knew he'd overstepped his bounds again.

But Susan smiled at him instead. "Look, Paul," she said, "I don't want to fight. I know this hasn't been easy for you."

"Easy for me?" he replied. "You're the one who's sick. I'm just in charge of complaining about it!" They both laughed.

We were the ring-around-the-rosy children
They were circles around the sun
Never give up, never slow down
Never grow old, never ever die young.
—JAMES TAYLOR FROM THE SONG "Never Die Young"

In 1958, San Pedro Boulevard was a busy four-lane highway that ran past Paul's family's white house through a Tampa, Florida, suburb straight to Tampa Bay. Paul and Susan had a small reddish brown dachshund they called Weenie. This was a wonderful little dog when he wasn't torturing water bugs on the hardwood floor. Paul loved that animal for the same reason almost everyone loved dogs…their affection was unconditional.

Weenie must have been a fish in his last lifetime. Whenever he could, he would bolt out the front door and run the three miles to the bay where he would stop and bark at the water until Paul's father drove there to pick him up. One Sunday evening, a knock at the door interrupted the Ed Sullivan show. The neighborhood bully had found Weenie lying whimpering in the street. With uncharacteristic kindness, he had wrapped the dog up in his jacket and carried him to Paul's house. Weenie took his last breaths only minutes before they arrived, but Paul remembered being comforted by the realization that his pet hadn't been alone when he died.

From a Buddhist view of eternal life, the first few hours immediately after someone dies are an extremely important time for loved ones to pray for the deceased's enlightenment. Paul understood the importance of making this cause and was determined to be with Susan at that moment if she didn't survive her illness.

> *Birds and crickets cry, but never shed tears. I, Nichiren, do not cry, but my tears flow ceaselessly.*
> —NICHIREN

Paul gently rubbed Susan's forehead as she lay on her back sleeping. She looks a lot like me, he thought. Even has no hair! He wondered if she had chanted any since he last saw her. He knew that was doubtful since she had so little strength left. He had been praying hard enough for both of them.

The door to the room opened quietly and Rob, Susan's boyfriend, walked in. Rob was tall and handsome. A successful professional, he commanded respect from everyone around him. Someone Paul's mother would have loved as a son-in-law if she hadn't already died from cancer herself. Still, in spite of his irritating perfection, Rob did love Paul's sister. He had to give him that. And, it wasn't as if Paul didn't have a successful career himself. It was just that Rob was so...*perfect*.

He nodded at Paul and sat down in the chair on the other side of the bed.

"Ah, hi, Rob," Paul mumbled.

Rob just nodded.

Paul, realizing he owed Rob an apology, forced himself to continue. "Hey, look, I'm real sorry I was so obnoxious last week. I had no right to talk that way."

"No problem. We're all under a lot of stress right now," Rob replied with a wistful look.

Both of them sat quietly and watched Susan sleep. Paul, who usually felt the need to fill silence with noise, actually felt comfortable not talking. Finally, he kissed his big sister on the forehead and, after touching Rob lightly on his shoulder, left.

> *And the cup that once appeared half empty*
> *has become a cup that is half full*
> *where there was a space there now is plenty*
> *you're a lucky sign ascending*
> *no one does for me what you do.*
> —BASIA FROM THE SONG "The Sweetest Illusion"

The evening shadows were beginning to invade the empty booths at Bea's Diner. Paul, still in faded jeans and looking rather distraught, sat across the last table from Kate. She was wearing a tweed business suit and decompressing from a busy workday. Her stuffed briefcase was on the bench next to her. She called over to Bea for a cup of coffee and stretched across the table to hold Paul's cold hands.

"How'd it go today?" she asked.

"Well, I chanted for more than two hours this morning before I went to the hospital, no one arrested me and I wasn't struck by lightning on the way, and Susan's boyfriend didn't try to operate on me."

Kate responded quickly. "You know, Paul. Self-pity just doesn't fit you. Where's the ol' gray clouds are gonna clear up fella I met before in this same diner?"

Before Paul could answer (assuming he even was going to), Bea, her gray hair in a net, placed a steaming mug in front of Kate. Looking over at Paul, she asked, "Someone run over your pet poodle, sport?"

"Oh, great. Two comedians for the price of one," Paul retorted.

Bea muttered under her breath loud enough for them to hear as she walked away, "Well, excuse me for living."

"You know, Paul," Kate said, "if you don't do something to change your outlook, you're not going to be of any use to Susan or, for that matter, yourself."

"I know. I'm having a difficult time accepting that Susan has to die. I mean, I understand it intellectually. But in my heart I just can't bear it." Kate handed him her napkin for the tears running down his face.

"I brought you an article to read." She pushed a magazine across the table. "It has a lecture by Daisaku Ikeda on one of Nichiren's letters to a mother who lost one of her young sons suddenly," she continued. "I thought it might help you make sense out of what you're going through."

Paul looked down at the article listlessly.

Kate sighed and, picking it up, read, "The impermanence of life is inescapable. In Buddhism, this is a fundamental premise about the nature of existence. Why should death come as a shock? From the standpoint of life's eternity, it could be said that birth and death are occurrences of minuscule significance. That is all well and good in theory, but the human heart cannot fully come to terms with such events through theory alone."

"See," she said, "it's what you were telling me a few months ago."

Looking slightly more interested, Paul said, "You know, after my parents died, I thought I had become an expert at this life and death thing. I mean, I know we're all going to die someday. But Susan's only forty-eight years old...it doesn't seem right."

"Have you been chanting about it?"

"Yeah, I have been." Paul whispered, tears streaming down his cheeks. "But, I'm so afraid of losing her."

"I know you are," she replied. "But, didn't you tell me about the impermanence of attachments? Doesn't that apply to people as well? None of us will be here forever."

"I know that. It's just that I somehow bought into the notion that a life—our lives—were supposed to last a certain number of years. You know, at least seventy-five or eighty years."

> *I have a mission—mine alone;*
> *You too have a mission only you can fulfill.*
> —Daisaku Ikeda

Kate placed her hand in his and said, "Paul, I don't think it's a question of how long we live but rather what we do with the years we have. You're the person who helped me see that we each have a unique mission. For some people that may take many years. But for others, only a few. Your sister is a remarkable person. And no matter how long her life is in years, I know she believes it has been a full and meaningful one."

From behind the counter, Bea quietly observed Paul take another step in his own personal journey to accept the inevitability of the cycle of life and death. Overhearing their conversation caused her to self-reflect as well. Finally, she carried her cup of coffee over to their table and sat down next to Kate, who looked over in surprise.

After taking a sip of her coffee, Bea said to Paul, "Sorry about your sister. I lost my youngest brother September 11. He was a firefighter."

Neither Paul nor Kate knew what to say, so they just waited for her to continue.

"I've thought a lot about his life and why he had to die." She dabbed her eye with a napkin and continued. "You know, I have to admit that sometimes I accidentally overhear your conversations about your Buddhist chanting."

"Only occasionally," she added.

Again, they waited. Not speaking.

"I don't understand how your chanting makes a difference in the world. I mean how can regular people like us stop this madness that is killing innocent people?"

Kate looked at Paul for him to answer.

In a quiet voice, he said, "Bea, these are really great questions. They go to the heart of our practice and faith.

The phrase we chant, Nam-myoho-renge-kyo, revolutionizes our lives, allowing us to manifest our enlightened nature. And because we are connected to everyone around us, each positive cause we make has a profound effect on the world."

Continuing, Paul added, "I've been personally struggling with why some people get to live to ninety and others only ten. But I'm just starting to realize that it isn't the quantity but the quality of our lives here on earth that matters. I don't know how long someone's life is supposed to be. Or mine for that matter."

"Well," Bea said, "clearly we have no control over when we die. Or my brother would still be alive. It's how we live each day that's important. That's why I insist on making the best chili dogs in America."

Kate and Paul chuckled. Then Paul said, "The three of us are a wonderful example of the basic concept of dependent origination—that we are all connected in some fundamental way to everyone else on the planet. That how we treat each person we meet is really important."

"I guess I can buy that," she interrupted.

Paul continued, "A change in our own life can have a great impact on the environment and people around us. Can we be completely happy as long as a single human being somewhere is still suffering? We believe our mission as Buddhists is to try each day to continue to develop our lives—to polish our enlightened nature to the best of our ability.

"When we chant, we are praying to activate the enlightened compassion within our lives so that we can positively react to events around us...even tragic ones. What's most important isn't that everyone chant but that as many people as possible reach out to bridge the differences between us."

"Okay," Bea responded. "I can understand how this chanting can affect your life. I've seen how much Kate has changed. But what I don't get is how it will make any difference in the grand scheme of things."

Kate leaned forward to reply, "Our chanting also activates the characteristics of responsibility, wisdom and compassion. Like Paul said, we first apply these factors to our own lives and then to our family and loved ones. And then further out in circles to everyone in the country and the world. It's through our actions...based on our increasing sense of responsibility, wisdom and compassion...that we can ultimately change the world."

Bea nodded her encouragement for Kate to continue.

"Even a small sincere discourse with someone or a small kind act can positively influence that person who might then positively impact another person and so on. It's up to each of us to decide which actions we want to take beyond our daily spiritual practice."

Paul added, "Some people say we are only six degrees of separation from everyone else on the planet. So each time you treat a customer with respect and engage in positive dialogue, you potentially have a tremendous impact on the future of world peace. This is why each human being is so important. And why each moment we live is precious. We will never accomplish world peace through physical might. It's only through dialogue and mutual respect that we can ultimately create a peaceful world."

Bea patted Paul's hand as she stood up and said, "You know, Paul. You're a lot less depressing than you were when you first came in tonight."

Kate looked up to Bea and said, "I'm sorry about your brother, Bea. You must really miss him. I think everyone will have their own views of the appropriateness of America's response to the terrible events of September 11. Some might see it as too violent. Others might view it as a necessary short-term self-defense against a terrible evil. I believe continual dialogue and respect is the only solution that will bring permanent joy and relief to the suffering people of the world."

"While our lives are eternal," Paul said, "our time here on earth is finite—we'll all die at some point. So rather than being overly afraid of these tragic events, we can be convinced that these difficult times are our opportunity to change our own personal karma and the destiny of all humanity. This is our mission. To do our human revolution and by doing this to send ripples of compassion out into the universe."

"And," Kate added, "that's the best way for you to give meaning to your brother's life."

"It all starts with us, doesn't it?" Bea mused as she walked behind the counter to help a new customer.

Neither Paul nor Kate felt the need to answer. Out the window they could see a half moon shining behind gray clouds. It perfectly suited their mood.

Happiness and Daily Life

Elevating My Life

The Buddhist analysis of the dynamics of life…
is more detailed and subtle than any modern Western
analysis that I know of.
—ARNOLD TOYNBEE FROM *Choose Life*

LIKE A DISCIPLINED herd of cattle, a few hundred
people left the circular conference room and
moved toward eight large elevators on the tenth floor of
the Federal Aviation Administration building on a blus-
tery Washington, D.C. winter afternoon in 1985.

I allowed myself to be pushed along, headed for the
first floor, then out to my car, and, assuming the Washington, D.C. rush-hour traffic cooperated, an early family dinner. Several other government and contractor
employees squeezed into the elevator after me. We had
all been at an annual FAA awards presentation. As my
division's marketing director, I was there to witness two
of my fellow company employees receive commenda-
tions for outstanding support to a critical computer
modernization project.

The doors slowly closed. I calculated the odds that
someone would get off on each floor and then berated
myself for being pessimistic. However, in my defense,

last summer a young girl visiting with her mother hit all the elevator buttons and contributed to my tardiness to a meeting with one of my most important clients on the tenth floor.

A burly, middle-aged man, with an elevator company logo and the name "Tom" embroidered in white thread on his blue overalls, entered just as the door closed. He was holding a small walkie-talkie into which he said, "Harve, I think we've finally fixed this one. I'll just ride the little hummer down to make sure." The response was unintelligible to all but him.

The elevator doors haltingly opened on the ninth floor. Bodhisattvas and children's toys, I wanted to say ...like a department store announcement. (Lately, I had been relating everything to the Buddhist concept of the Ten Worlds. Both my daughters were becoming quite annoyed with this!) What should have been called out was ninth floor, last chance to another lift.

The floor of the elevator was misaligned with the hallway by about a foot. Two short men engaged in intense conversation stepped up and out as if nothing was wrong. I heard the repairman mumble something under his breath, "Hmm...maybe one more floor will fix it." "Oh, no," I thought.

We screeched to a halt somewhere between the eighth and ninth floors. Eighth floor, I thought. Must contain the eighth world of realization —a state in which one seeks the truth through one's own direct perception of phenomena. In this case, the realization was that we were stuck!

A middle-aged and very upset manager (one of the few I didn't enjoy dealing with) said to the repairman, "Hey, you! Get me off this elevator right now. I have a four o'clock meeting with the administrator."

(Ha! Must have been getting off at the fourth floor, the world of anger.)

"No problem," Tom replied. "I'll just call Harve and he'll switch to override and take us down a floor. No problem."

"It's okay to have problems," I piped in. "It's overcoming them that's concerning us."

Everyone laughed nervously . . . even him.

While Tom intensely spoke "elevatorese" with good ol' Harve, one of the passengers responded that the difficulty for her was finding wisdom when she was too upset to see straight. I hadn't noticed that my close friend and colleague, Anne, was on the elevator on the other side of a group of people. Anne was also a Buddhist and could be disarmingly honest. She squeezed her way over to us and said, "I can sure relate. That's why it's so important that we find a way to tap that inner wisdom or oneness with the ultimate truth that exists in each of us."

Inner wisdom and the ultimate truth...the tenth world of Buddhahood. Should have brought that with me when I first got on. Wait a minute...I did bring it! I started quietly chanting Nam-myoho-renge-kyo for the world of Buddhahood to well up and manifest itself in the other nine worlds. Then I watched in awe as Tom, distracted up to then with technical issues, stopped to ask if anyone wanted something from the cafeteria since we might be stuck here for an hour or so.

Simple orders were placed and snacks sent down the elevator shaft through a small maintenance hatch. All right, thanks to Tom, we replaced the second world of hunger with the ninth world of Bodhisattva—a compassionate action that relieves the sufferings of others and the sixth world of heaven—a state of short-lived joy. Two worlds for the price of one! (Strange that the FAA cafeteria, focal point of so much hunger, was actually on the second floor.)

I overheard Tom speaking again into the tiny speaker. "Check page ninety-eight of the service manual," he was pleading. "I think it'll show you the correct wiring."

I wisely swallowed a "little-late-to-be-returning-to-the-world-of-elevator-learning, isn't it, Tom?" comment. I complimented myself on exercising better judgment through reason, a characteristic of the fifth world of humanity.

Ten nervous people in a cramped space generated considerable body heat. That and the uncertainty of our situation threatened to cause tempers to flare. A young mother with an adorable newborn in a carrier summed up everyone's feeling with, "This is hell!"

Another lady quickly responded, "Actually, this is just another of life's tests that will determine whether we go to heaven or hell after we die."

Anne gave me her patented please-Mike-just-let-it-drop-don't-make-things-worse look. But it was hot and

I was bored, so I remarked, "You know, ma'am, for many years, people thought of hell as a distinct place or unbearably hot region where people were tormented."

Tom, who was obviously upset at the failure of his co-workers to rapidly repair the elevator, said, "Right now all I can think of is frustration."

Anne said, "Well, that's a sort of hellish condition. But the amazing thing is that as soon as this elevator starts moving again, you'll be filled with rapturous joy—the sixth world of heaven."

The mother asked, "What are these worlds and who thought them up?"

"Excellent question," I answered. "The concept of the Ten Worlds evolved during the last three thousand years, originally from the teachings of Shakyamuni or Siddhartha, the historical Buddha. Later, as Buddhism from India spread through China to Japan, a man named Nichiren, born in the thirteenth century, gave a more practical expression to this Buddhist philosophy of life and used it to describe the lives of common people...it was like putting a scientific principle to work."

"So, I give up," a young, sandy-haired engineer said. "What are these Ten Worlds?"

I looked at Anne for help since I usually forgot one of the worlds or the correct order. She bailed me out with a smug look. Counting on her fingers, she ticked off all ten.

"Hell, hunger, animality, anger, humanity, heaven, learning, realization, bodhisattva and Buddhahood."

"Nothing personal, dearie," interjected a gray-haired, elderly lady who was wearing a thin hair net, "but most of the world's major religions have a concept of life flowing from one emotion to another."

"True," I said, "but Nichiren Buddhism differs in that it not only describes how our life changes from moment to moment but how it follows a discernible pattern with each event linked in a cause and effect relationship."

"So," asked Tom, "you mean that at any moment I might go into one of the other nine worlds? What if I don't want to?"

I answered, "Do you mean, how can we positively influence our environment instead of our surroundings dictating how we're feeling?"

He nodded.

"That's the beauty of this philosophy," Anne answered. By now, people had figured out that we were friends. "It answers the question most of us are desperately asking, 'How can I be happy?' I mean, let's face it. For a religion or philosophy to be really useful to people everywhere, regardless of race or nationality or social standing, doesn't it have to give each person the ability to leave a lower life-condition of life, say hell, for a higher, more productive condition, like learning?"

"Wait a minute," interrupted the young mother. "I have an older child at home who still requires constant supervision. So don't give me some theory about how I should never get angry. And, by the way, my husband is unemployed, so pardon me if I pray for a little simple material fulfillment next year." She was on the verge of tears and was visibly distressed.

Everyone was silent for a few moments. Just feeling her misery seemed to evoke a compassionate or bodhisattva reaction. I said, very quietly, "You're absolutely correct to point that out. We will never eliminate the nine worlds. Our challenge is to draw forth the power and insight of the tenth world of Buddhahood or enlightenment so that the other nine worlds fall into the correct perspective and work toward our own and others' happiness. By influencing the nine worlds and expressing the positive aspects in each one, we can call forth positive reactions from the environment and society."

I went on to add, "We'll always have problems...and it's often easier to blame them on someone else. But if we're not careful, we'll become like the fish that are tricked by the fisherman's bait and destroyed. By understanding how we normally react to the environment— our basic life tendency—by tapping the tenth world of Buddhahood and by taking responsibility for our own problems, we can begin to radically improve our lives."

"Then, I guess happiness," Tom contributed, "isn't an absence of problems but rather being able to successfully navigate our way through them."

Everyone nodded in agreement, including the upset lady.

With a sigh of relief, I felt the elevator jerk and begin its overdue descent. Anne and I walked wearily through the empty lobby sharing our amazement at our difficult but rewarding experience.

I felt very fortunate to have found this Buddhism. I said out loud, "Sure am glad we were finally able to elevate our life-conditions!"

Anne groaned.

Holiday Identity Crisis

With an American Jewish heritage, a Buddhist practice and two young daughters, what holidays to celebrate in 1987 became an important question.

It was early Christmas morning
And all over my house,
Not a creature was stirring,
Not even a mouse.
I tiptoed downstairs
Past the first sunlight beam,
Took a look at our family room
And let out a scream!

My daughters came running,
My wife tumbled out.
Together they queried me...
Why such a shout?
We have both a menorah and
Christmas tree, I cried.
Oh, oh, said my family
His brain must be fried.

It's not my brain I insisted,
But something we missed.
Something to do with
Being a Buddhist.
I know what it isn't, but I'm not
Sure what it is.
And so we decided
To get down to biz.

We searched through Nichiren's letters
And Daisaku Ikeda's writings,
And tried to reach a consensus
With a minimum of fighting.
As we chanted, I thought
What an emotional issue,
But I'll bet our faith deepens
Before we are through.

DECEMBER has always been a confusing time of year for me. Both my wife and I have a Jewish heritage and, especially for her, Hanukkah has been a significant holiday. I, on the other hand, have always been a sucker for Christmas. I love the tree, the stockings, the eggnog, the songs, the eggnog (did I mention eggnog?).

Our daughters have had different feelings depending on their age. But, in general, I'd have to say they like the presents—both giving and receiving—especially when

Hanukkah arrives in early December and they make out like bandits!

They still love leaving cookies and milk for Santa Claus, even though they know I'm trying not to gain weight. Myself, I'm partial to mistletoe; I carry it around with me in case I unexpectedly run into my wife.

This holiday confusion is especially perplexing to my children. Friends who most likely celebrate Hanukkah or Christmas surround them at school. Of course, my daughters realize that we celebrate our joy of life with morning and evening chanting, but that's tough to explain to a group of classmates. And many of our family's social relationships in December, both through work and home, center on holiday activities. Avoiding them doesn't seem consistent with practicing Buddhism in our daily lives. Actually, it seems more like narrow-mindedness.

The most relevant Buddhist concept we uncovered to assist in solving our holiday dilemma was a precept called "adapting to local customs." According to *The Soka Gakkai Dictionary of Buddhism*, it means, "In matters the Buddha did not expressly either permit or forbid, one may act in accordance with local custom, so long as the fundamental principles of Buddhism are not violated."

So there must be a difference between the religious and cultural significance of the holiday season. We decided that this would be our barometer in judging the appropriateness of our holiday activities. Let me add that I don't believe this is a black and white issue. After all, faith is a lifetime journey. So each year, our perspective of ourselves as Buddhists changes. Some traditions that we have previously adhered to may now seem inappropriate while others are deemed acceptable.

Buddhism talks about the Middle Way. I think we have an obligation to our children to teach them the importance of achieving a balance in their lives. It must be difficult for a child to grow up without having experienced the warmth and fun of a holiday season. On the other hand, an overabundance of materialism that so often accompanies December can also be misleading.

Last night at dinner, our family decided not to have a Christmas tree this year but to fill small stockings on Christmas instead. We'll keep the Jewish menorah during Hanukkah for its cultural significance and because the girls enjoy lighting candles. We also resolved to fill December with helping others through our Buddhist, family, school and work activities.

> *Above on our rooftop,*
> *Several reindeer hoofs pounded.*
> *We gathered around our altar*
> *As the prayer bell sounded.*
> *The four of us huddled—*
> *World peace seemed so near.*
> *And to all—a good night*
> *And a life full of cheer.*

The Elusive There

....

Much of the difficulty in discerning the workings of good and evil is due to our unwillingness to acknowledge the potential of both supreme good and evil within our own lives.
—FROM *Living Buddhism*

As a youngster growing up in Los Angeles, I defined "good" as a Baby Ruth candy bar and a large bottle of RC Cola. "Bad" was anyone I didn't like or who treated me poorly. As I got older, I subconsciously continued to label many of the events and people in my life as either being good or bad, comfortable or uncomfortable. More than half a century later, as a supposed adult, it amazes me how much I still do this!

I have been making a concerted effort during the last few years to accept my life, as it is, both good and bad, instead of obsessing about how I wish it would be. In the past, I spent considerable energy trying to reach an elusive "there," "there" meaning everything "good"—a better job, a more pleasant boss or just a little more money. It was almost impossible to enjoy life as it was when I was so busy wishing I were somewhere else.

A key aspect of a healthy Buddhist perspective is the realization that we are exactly where we need to be for our own human revolution. The belief that our happiness depends on some event or situation happening in the future actually sets us up for unhappiness. Especially when we consider that we are all bound by the cycle of birth, aging, sickness and death. So if we wait for a trouble-free life, our happiness will continue to elude us.

I am also continuing to work on how I relate to other people, especially individuals who give me grief. Many people I know have a tendency to simply label someone who does something "bad" as being a "bad" person or something even more descriptive. But this isn't consistent with Nichiren's assertion that each human being is a Buddha with all the Ten Worlds and, so, worthy of our respect. As long as we continue to judge others to the extreme, then there can never be world peace.

When I get upset with someone for something they have done or said, I now try to reflect on that specific behavior instead of declaring the individual unworthy. By awakening my compassion for that person as a fellow human, I am able to communicate my concern without going into attack mode. This was very effective with a client of mine. Her demanding management style was preventing her key staff from feeling free to express their opinions. Finally, when her behavior started to upset me as well, I realized I needed to have a dialogue with her.

First, I chanted with the understanding that it was her behavior that was the problem, not her as a human being. Later, after I had a productive discussion with my client, she actually thanked me profusely for pointing out why her actions were not consistent with her desired company culture. And, instead of canceling my contract, the next day, she invited my wife and me out to dinner! This breakthrough was only made possible by transforming my initial negative judgment into a constructive dialogue.

I have been slowly accepting that I have an enlightened condition within my life, as does everyone else. This has helped me have more compassion for my family, friends, clients and myself. As a minor added benefit, I no longer feel the need to look over my shoulder when I sneak an occasional Baby Ruth bar!

It's Not Always a Laughing Matter

....

L AST WEEK, Don, the engineer, wandered up to me just as I was hanging up the phone. Don doesn't walk…he mopes. He doesn't laugh…he grunts. This is a guy who takes the Three Stooges seriously.

I tried my usual joke of the day routine to no avail and then, deciding to pull out all the stops, put on the fake mustache and eyeglasses I usually reserve for going-away parties. No luck. Apparently, for Don, humor just wasn't a laughing matter.

Phew, I thought. Even taciturn Ralph from accounting, who started chanting a few months earlier, was beginning to see the humor in things. I left the office that night determined to search out some deeper perspectives on humor so I could lift Don's spirits before he sank into terminal depression.

First, I scoured my own memories for humorous occurrences. Let's see…there was the time at a bicentennial parade in New York in 1976 when I inadvertently led all the VIPs in their sports cars past the reviewing stand where they should have been dropped off. I had to part marching bands as I led them back three blocks to where they belonged. Later that evening, this was good for a resounding ten-minute belly laugh. And, considering it was the culmination of a year of preparation, a welcome stress relief.

I then talked to my good friend, Joe. He had just bought a new mobile telephone whose primary function seemed to be to generate static during the most intense conversational moments. We both felt (crackle, crackle) that Daisaku Ikeda's humorous references and interplay with those on the stage and in the audience at a recent Buddhist meeting spoke volumes about the importance of keeping our problems in perspective. He seemed to be saying, "World peace is a lifetime journey...so, take it one step at a time." In the midst of all our struggles, it's important to remember to enjoy our lives.

Joe then quoted science fiction author Robert Heinlein (crackle, crackle), who once said that humor is a courageous form of sharing. We reflected that great leaders, whom we respect, always seem to reach out to everyone they meet, regardless of their social status or personal challenges. They often use humor, not necessarily to be funny, but to lighten heavy hearts...to give hope. We agreed the world needs many more leaders with this kind of attitude...with the ability to encourage people like my workmate Don and lift his (crackle) spirits.

My elderly friend, Elizabeth, was watching *Star Trek, the Next Generation*, when I called, so I only bothered her for a few minutes. But, as usual, that was more than enough. She said that a joke made only to solicit a laugh or make fun of others rarely penetrates a person's heart or creates anything of value. Humor that stems from compassion, on the other hand, can be an effective way of establishing trust in a non-offensive manner. This type of humor can provide the bridge over which more serious ideas and concerns can travel. She then told me to live long and prosper and returned to her television show.

Later that evening, I recalled attending a student lecture on Buddhism at UCLA that was given by Daisaku Ikeda in 1974. He drew a triangle on the blackboard and labeled it the "small ego." This, he said, was our own life. He then drew a much larger triangle that enclosed the smaller one. He labeled it the "large ego" and explained that it represented everything we did to relieve the suffering of others. He pointed out that when we took care of the larger ego, then the needs of the smaller ego, our own happiness, were also fulfilled.

This also reminded me that it is the life of the Buddha within that we tap when we chant that will enable us to make the most effective use of humor in our relations with others. This has definitely been my challenge over the years as I have struggled with my strange sense of humor. Like most things, it has proven to be both a strength and a weakness depending on how and when I choose to employ it. When I was younger, I too often tried to be funny when the person I was talking to wanted to discuss something serious. I now use humor much less to distance myself from others and more as a way to get closer to people. And, according to Don, that's no laughing matter.

What Is Happiness?

....

There is no true happiness for human beings other than chanting Nam-myoho-renge-kyo.

—Nichiren

THE WORD *happy* has numerous interpretations. Many people think of happy as meaning always cheerful, always in high spirits. But it is probably a misconception to expect to be in high spirits all the time just because we're practicing Buddhism. I sometimes worry that when I and others in our Buddhist community use the word, we might lead people to believe that if they chant Nam-myoho-renge-kyo they will be "happy" in this sense all the time. I wonder if we should find another way—a different expression—to define our goal.

When I joined the SGI, my wife and I were hippies. We had run away from home in 1969 seeking love, peace, happiness and, in my case, freedom from responsibility. After months of eating brown rice and lentils and living on a friend's porch, we realized that we couldn't just survive on our ideals. Buddhism seemed like the perfect solution.

We were told that if we chanted, we could become

happy and all our dreams would come true. So we taught ourselves how to recite part of the Lotus Sutra while sitting every day in a West Los Angeles park and soon began to build a more constructive life together. After many years of practice, we built incredibly good fortune in our lives and acquired a deep sense of gratitude for our Buddhist community.

I rarely thought to ask what happiness was. I figured anything would be better than the severe depression and anguish I had suffered as a child and teenager.

Because of my intense desire to avoid depression, I developed an underlying belief that my true objective through my practice was to be happy all the time. That the enlightenment Nichiren spoke about was somehow wrapped up in an unshakable condition of happiness, a total absence of pain. "Look at me," I would be able to proclaim. "Nothing can upset my positive, upbeat attitude."

And so I expended a tremendous amount of energy trying to maintain this condition. I actually got to the point where I knew exactly how much to chant each day to "stay happy." People came to expect and rely on my perpetual smile and good humor.

I was so frightened whenever I started to feel blue that I would do anything to get my smile back. Much of my chanting was centered (and self-centered) on staying in high spirits, as opposed to more significant prayers. Deep inside, I still had a lot of sadness and hurt. I had yet to understand what true happiness meant.

In retrospect, this misconception was probably exactly what I needed through my twenties and thirties to allow me to build a positive marriage, family and career. My unhappiness, like a strong ocean undertow, was a constant impetus to chant more to strengthen my life. Because of it, I lifted myself above my unstable childhood. But, on a different level, I still needed to deal with the reality of my sadness.

In the summer of 1997, with my wife's serious illness as an additional pressure, I found myself no longer able to contain the misery. I couldn't keep it in its box. I became overwhelmed with grief. Fortunately, I sought professional help.

Through therapy and a reinvigorated study of Nichiren's writings, I started to realize that it was important to allow myself to experience my sadness and anger. Much of my adult behavior was patterned after negative childhood experiences and realities that were no longer valid. What a relief to realize that it was okay to be sad sometimes. That the fact that I might not be feeling happy at a given moment did not necessarily indicate that my practice was weak or my faith shallow! I finally began to accept and love myself—for the first time in my life.

By happy, I think Nichiren meant something close to the joy or sense of fulfillment that arises from the realization that we are truly living in the moment, the confidence that comes from our sense of mission and the ability to enjoy our life. Being happy is a sense of connectedness with everything around us.

The words we use to describe the positive results of our Buddhist practice are important. I realize we don't really believe that if people chant, they will always be smiling and cheerful. Rather, they will be more fulfilled and happy with their lives. Still, it's probably important that we remind ourselves that the objective of our Buddhist practice—of our life, is not to be smiling all the time. True happiness comes from within and is a condition we can experience even when we're facing difficulties.

I had a really bad cold last week. At the same time, I found myself filled with joy as my wife and I celebrated our wedding anniversary. Was I happy last week? Not really. On a physical level I felt miserable. But on a deeper level I felt extremely fulfilled.

Anyway, I hope someone will suggest a different word for this state of life, one that won't unintentionally confuse some people or possibly even cause them to be unhappy. Such a word would make me very [insert word for happy].

Reference

A Brief Introduction to Nichiren Buddhism

N ICHIREN BUDDHISM offers teachings for personal and social transformation. This begins with people taking responsibility for their own lives and gradually projecting their increased wisdom, courage and compassion into their surroundings.

Nichiren Daishonin's Buddhism is a life philosophy based on the fundamental belief that all humans have an enlightened or Buddha nature within their life. Buddha means an "Awakened One"...not a special or supernatural being, but a potential any person can realize. Nichiren taught that the key to unlocking this unlimited wisdom and fortune is to chant the phrase *Nam-myoho-renge-kyo*. It was Nichiren's desire, based on his deep concern for the happiness and welfare of all people, to make the essential truths of Buddhism accessible to everyone. He predicted that as more and more people embraced this humanistic philosophy, overcame their sufferings and had their lives filled with compassion and purpose, world peace would be achieved.

The son of a Japanese fisherman, Nichiren (1222–1282) left home at an early age to study at various temples. He exhaustively scrutinized all the Buddhist sutras (teachings) and finally became convinced that the Lotus Sutra was the highest of these teachings. Many Buddhist scholars and practitioners now agree with his conclusion.

The twenty-eight chapter Lotus Sutra presents itself as a written record of the oral teachings of the first recorded Buddha, Shakyamuni (also called Gautama or Siddartha). Born in India about twenty-five hundred years ago, Shakyamuni renounced his wealth and status and dedicated his life to finding a solution to human suffering. Through dialogue, he established a connection with every person he encountered and employed a variety of teaching methods to lead them to an understanding of the eternity of life, the meaning of life and death and the correct attitude to obtain enlightenment.

He treated every individual with great respect and compassion. Enlightenment is an awakening to the true nature of life, including the profound realization of the interconnectedness of all things—the inseparable relationship between the individual and the environment and the ability of each human being to powerfully influence both. This realization leads individuals to assume personal responsibility for their own condition of life and the environment around them.

After Shakyamuni's death, Buddhism spread from India to China along the Silk Road and, eventually, to Japan over the next thousand years. In China, T'ien'tai expounded the theory of three thousand realms in a single moment of life, which he formulated based on the Lotus Sutra. The core of his philosophy is the concept of the Ten Worlds or conditions of life. Loosely defined, these are hell, hunger, animality, anger, humanity, heaven, learning, realization, bodhisattva and Buddhahood. (A more detailed description is provided in the glossary.)

Every moment we manifest the characteristics of the first nine worlds. Different events in our environment cause us to react according to one of these conditions. The most important objective for our own happiness is to be able to tap into the tenth world of Buddhahood— to make it our fundamental response to whatever happens in our life.

Attaining Buddhahood does not mean becoming a special being. In this state, one still continues to work against and defeat the negative functions of life and transform any and all difficulty into causes for further development. It is a state of complete access to the boundless wisdom, compassion, courage and other qualities inherent in life. With these, one can create harmony with and among others and between human life and nature.

Early Buddhist schools emphasized a monastic lifestyle. They taught their disciples that the path to enlightenment required detaching themselves from all earthly desires and mastering complex doctrines. Needless to say, this method of achieving enlightenment was only open to a small percentage of society. Most people didn't have the luxury of escaping their daily life. Nichiren, on the other hand, taught his followers that the path to enlightenment was through directly living in society.

Buddhism also speaks of the concept of karma...that the causes we make (both good and bad) accumulate over countless lifetimes and define the reality of our present existence. The theories of karma and the three thousand realms in a single moment of life are very profound and deserve considerably more attention than can be given here. However, the most important point is to recognize that who we are today is the sum total of all the causes we have made in the past and who we will be in the future will depend on the causes we are presently making. So, it is important to ask ourselves, "What is the highest cause we can make today for our own happiness and the happiness of others?"

> *Even though one neither reads nor studies the sutra, chanting the title alone is the source of tremendous good fortune. The sutra teaches that women, evil men, and those in the realms of animals and hell—in fact, all the beings of the Ten Worlds—can attain Buddhahood in their present form.*
> —NICHIREN

Nichiren explained that the highest cause—the essence of thousands of Buddhist sutras—was contained within the title of the Lotus Sutra (Myoho-renge-kyo). He appended the word for devotion, *nam*, and taught that by invoking the phrase *Nam-myoho-renge-kyo*, human beings could tap into their inherent wisdom and display the characteristics of an enlightened being in this lifetime as opposed to having to wade through countless existences to finally reach this state.

Nam-myoho-renge-kyo is pronounced as follows:

Nam—the *a* has the sound of the *a* in *father*
Myo—think of it as placing an *m* before one-half
 of *yo-yo*
Ho—like the garden implement *hoe*
Ren—like the bird *wren*
Ge—sounds like the word *get* without the *t*
Kyo—similar to *myo*

Each syllable gets one equal stress or beat: Nám myó hó rén gé kyó.

We react to someone calling out our name even if they know nothing about us. Similarly, if we say the phrase *Nam-myoho-renge-kyo*, our internal enlightened nature responds. At any given moment, we have the key within our own lives to unlock our Buddha nature...a revolutionary concept.

Loosely translated, *nam* means fusion with or devotion to. Viewed from the perspective of the eternity of life, happiness that is solely based on fame, wealth or position is fleeting. A much more unshakable joy can be achieved by fusing our life with the Law of Myoho-renge-kyo, the ultimate Law of life.

Myoho is the Mystic Law, the ultimate reality that is beyond our ability to perceive but is still true. Like the law of gravity, Myoho-renge-kyo functions as a universal truth regardless of our understanding or awareness of it.

Renge is Japanese for the lotus flower, which signifies the simultaneous nature of cause and effect. It is one of the few plants in nature in which flower and fruit appear at the same time. When our lives reach a stalemate…a serious work or relationship problem, for instance…a natural tendency is be overcome with grief, unable to move ahead. Buddhism teaches that if we chant instead, the effect of enlightenment will appear immediately in our life and, over time, visibly manifest itself as tremendous benefit. The beautiful lotus flower grows out of a muddy swamp. This is a metaphor for the beautiful lives we can create by overcoming our problems.

Kyo has been translated as both "sutra," the teaching of a Buddha, and "sound." By chanting (reciting out loud) Nam-myoho-renge-kyo, we are placing our lives in harmony or rhythm with this Law and with the universe.

What about the effect of outside influences on our lives? Don't the environment, our upbringing and other societal influences mold who we are? To some degree, this is true. However, at a much deeper level, Buddhism teaches that our lives are like a magnet. We attract either fortune or misfortune in strict accordance with the causes we have made.

Our lives and our environment are like a body and its shadow. Only by straightening the body (our lives) can the shadow (our environment) be straightened (improved). We are responsible for what happens to us. So by changing ourselves, we can improve any situation, overcome any problem. Nichiren's Buddhism empowers us to reach our full potential as human beings, to do our human revolution.

> *If the minds of living beings are impure, their land is also impure, but if their minds are pure, so is their land. There are not two lands, pure or impure in themselves. The difference lies solely in the good or evil of our minds.*
> —NICHIREN

On April 28, 1253, Nichiren first chanted Nam-myoho-renge-kyo. Rather than adopt a passive scholarly lifestyle, Nichiren actively set out to convince others of the importance of embracing this humanistic life philosophy to eliminate the misfortune—disease, strife and starvation—that plagued Japan at the time. He was greatly persecuted by others who felt threatened by his teachings. He was exiled twice for extended periods in horrible conditions and was almost beheaded. However, in spite of these tremendous difficulties, he won countless debates and gained numerous converts.

Nichiren inscribed the physical manifestation of his enlightenment in a mandala called the Gohonzon. *Go* means true, fundamental or highest and *honzon* means object of devotion. Individual Gohonzon are enshrined in the homes of members and in community centers. The Gohonzon is a mirror to our Buddha nature and over time, through our practice, our life begins to reflect this enlightened condition.

The daily practice of Nichiren's Buddhism includes chanting Nam-myoho-renge-kyo and reciting a portion of the Lotus Sutra each morning and evening; studying the philosophy; and sharing it with others. Nichiren also taught that exerting ourselves in school and work, building harmony in our families and with others and developing our character are also integral to the practice of his teaching.

Many positive changes, such as better health, a happier family and an improved financial situation are seen early in one's practice. More fundamental changes—increased wisdom, good fortune and a youthful state of life—develop over many years.

The hundreds of letters Nichiren wrote to his disciples provide a clear explanation of his life philosophy. His warm words of encouragement reflect an insight into human nature and a deep compassion for the common person. His teachings were preserved for more than seven hundred years by a small number of believers. The Soka Gakkai, (Value-Creating Society), inherited this tradition in 1930. The Soka Gakkai was founded by Tsunesaburo Makiguchi, an educator who embraced

Nichiren's Buddhism as he pursued his goal of transforming Japanese society through the overhaul of its educational system.

Makiguchi and his disciple, Josei Toda, were imprisoned by the World War II Japanese military government for refusing to compromise their practice of Nichiren's Buddhism in favor of State Shintoism and also for resolutely denouncing the Japanese military's aggressions. Although seventy-two at the time of his imprisonment, Makiguchi was unswayed by his persecution and continued to try to reason with his interrogators. Despite the cruel stress of the prison hardships, he maintained his composure and dignity until the last moment of his life. He died in prison at age seventy-three. Toda emerged from jail determined to validate Makiguchi's beliefs that a value-creating organization that adhered to the humanistic strategy of the Lotus Sutra could transform our world.

Under Toda's direction, the lay organization grew to more than 750,000 families by the time of Toda's death in 1958. Thousands of families whose lives were practically destroyed as a result of the war were able to overcome immense financial, health and spiritual problems. Mr. Toda once stated that he could not be truly happy as long as a single person in the world was suffering. It was with this spirit that he continued his struggle to encourage everyone he met until the last moment of his life. A young man, Daisaku Ikeda, determined to learn from

Toda because he deeply admired and trusted Toda's commitment to peace and the elimination of all nuclear weapons.

Daisaku Ikeda became the third president of the Soka Gakkai in 1960 and is now president of the Soka Gakkai International. Mr. Ikeda has traveled to more than fifty countries in an unceasing campaign to build bridges of peace with people of all walks of life. In forty-five years, the organization has spread to more than 190 countries and territories with more than twelve million members. Mr. Ikeda, a writer, poet, philosopher and photographer, continues to travel worldwide encouraging individual members, delivering lectures at universities and holding dialogues with international authors, scholars and political leaders.

In his 1994 Peace Proposal to the United Nations, he said, "Symbiosis, which means living and prospering together, has become the key word of our time, whether in reference to the relationship between nations or that between humankind and nature. What is needed now is a 'total revolution for symbiosis,' which can be achieved only through a human revolution on a global scale."

The continuous process of polishing our lives through overcoming the problems we face is called human revolution. It is this process—individuals helping each other to revolutionize their own lives, as opposed to violent political or cultural revolution—that will lead to a harmonious world.

The SGI in the United States has almost ninety community and activity centers. Discussion meetings are conducted monthly in private homes where practicing members and friends study the philosophy and share their experiences of faith.

The SGI's Charter expresses the organization's philosophical tenets. In general, these guidelines express a strong desire to contribute to world peace through the unique culture and education of our communities, to protect the freedom of religious expression and respect for human rights and to cultivate the virtues of wisdom and compassion throughout the world as a method of resolving conflict. Following these guidelines and doing their inner human revolution, SGI members continue to reach out to others to create a more harmonious and peaceful world.

Selected Bibliography

These are some of the books I quoted from when writing this book. Please consult these books if you want more information about Nichiren Buddhism.

Galtung, Johan and Daisaku Ikeda. *Choose Peace*. London: Pluto Press, 1995.

Hochswender, Woody, Greg Martin and Ted Morino. *The Buddha in Your Mirror: Practical Buddhism and the Search for Self*. Santa Monica, CA: Middleway Press, 2001.

Ikeda, Daisaku. *The Creative Family*. Tokyo: NSIC, 1977.

———. *Discussions on Youth*, volume 1. Santa Monica, CA: World Tribune Press, 1998.

———. *Faith Into Action*. Santa Monica, CA: World Tribune Press, 1999.

———. *For the Sake of Peace: Seven Paths to Global Harmony, A Buddhist Perspective*. Santa Monica, CA: Middleway Press, 2001.

———. *For Today & Tomorrow*. Santa Monica, CA: World Tribune Press: 1999.

————. *Unlocking the Mysteries of Birth and Death…and Everything in Between*. Santa Monica, CA: Middleway Press, 2003.

————. *The Way of Youth: Buddhist Common Sense for Handling Life's Questions*. Santa Monica, CA: Middleway Press, 2000.

Living Buddhism magazine. Santa Monica, CA: SGI-USA Publications.

Soka Gakkai. *The Writings of Nichiren Daishonin*. Tokyo: Soka Gakkai, 1999.

Soka Gakkai. *The Soka Gakkai Dictionary of Buddhism*. Tokyo: Soka Gakkai, 2002.

Toynbee, Arnold and Daisaku Ikeda. *Choose Life, A Dialogue*. New York: Oxford University Press, 1976.

Watson, Burton. *The Lotus Sutra*. New York: Columbia University Press, 1993.

World Tribune newspaper. Santa Monica, CA: SGI-USA Publications.

Middleway Press books are available through your favorite neighborhood or On-line bookstore, or at: www.middlewaypress.org

World Tribune Press and other books available at SGI-USA bookstores nationwide, or at www.sgi-usa.org

Issues of the *Living Buddhism* magazine and the *World Tribune* newspaper are available at www.sgisubs.com

Glossary

Based on The Soka Gakkai Dictionary of Buddhism
(Tokyo, Soka Gakkai, 2002). Excerpted with permission.

Buddhism and Buddha—Buddhism is the name given to the teachings of the first historical Buddha (see Shakyamuni). In other words, Buddhism refers to all the sutras which Shakyamuni Buddha expounded in what is today called India in approximately 500 BCE.

Nichiren's teachings (thirteenth century Japan) are referred to as the Buddhism of sowing, in contrast with the earlier teachings of Shakyamuni, which are called the Buddhism of the harvest. The Buddhism of the harvest is that which can lead to enlightenment only for those who received the seeds of Buddhahood by practicing the Buddha's teachings in previous lifetimes. In contrast, the Buddhism of sowing implants the seeds of Buddhahood, or Nam-myoho-renge-kyo, in the lives of those who had no connection with the Buddha in their past existences.

The Buddha can in no way be defined as a transcendental or supreme being. "Buddha" means the Enlightened One; a Buddha is a person who perceives within his own life the essence or reality of life. This ultimate reality supports and nourishes humanity and all other living beings. Those who have perceived this ultimate reality inherent in their own lives truly know themselves; they are Buddhas.

cause and effect—Buddhism expounds the law of cause and effect that operates in life, ranging over past, present and future existences. This causality underlies the doctrine of karma. From this viewpoint, causes formed in the past are manifested as effects in the present. Causes formed in the present will be manifested as effects in the future. Buddhism emphasizes the causes one creates and accumulates in the present, because these will determine one's future. Nichiren taught that ordinary persons could manifest their innate Buddhahood (effect) through faith and practice, and then, based on Buddhahood, go out among the people of the nine worlds (cause) to lead them to Buddhahood.

Daisaku Ikeda—The third president of the Soka Gakkai and the current president of the Soka Gakkai International, is a Buddhist thinker, author and educator who believes that only through personal interaction and dialogue across cultural and philosophical boundaries can human beings nurture the trust and understanding that is necessary for lasting peace. To date, he has traveled to more than fifty countries in pursuit of this ideal, holding discussions with many distinguished political, cultural and educational figures. Topics include a range of issues crucial to humanity such as the transformative value of religion, the universality of life, social responsibility and sustainable progress and development.

eternity of life—Buddhism's view of eternal life posits that one's life or essence has no real beginning or end. We live many lifetimes, repeating the cycle of birth and death. Like going to sleep at night, we refresh our bodies and wake up anew in circumstances that correspond to our karma (see karma). It is extremely fortunate to be born as a human being with the potential to improve our own life while contributing to the happiness of those around us.

Gohonzon—Nichiren Daishonin inscribed a mandala, the fundamental object of respect called the Gohonzon, on October 12, 1279. This object, in the form of a scroll, depicts, in Chinese characters, Nam-myoho-renge-kyo (the Law) and the life of Nichiren (the Person), as well as protective influences. Down the center of the Gohonzon are the characters *Nam-myoho-renge-kyo* and Nichiren's signature. This indicates the oneness of Person and Law—that the condition of Buddhahood is a potential within and can be manifested by all people. SGI members enshrine a replica of the original Gohonzon in their homes as a focal point for their daily practice. The Gohonzon's power comes from the practitioner's faith—the Gohonzon functions as a spiritual mirror. Sitting in front of the Gohonzon and chanting, a person is able to recognize and reveal his or her own Buddha nature, the creative essence of life.

human revolution—*Human revolution* was a term used by Josei Toda, second president of the Soka Gakkai, to describe the process by which individuals gradually expand their lives, conquer their negative and destructive tendencies and ultimately make the state of Buddhahood their dominant life-condition. SGI President Daisaku Ikeda wrote the following words in the foreword to his novel *The Human Revolution*, "A great human revolution in just a single individual will help achieve a change in the destiny of a nation and further, will enable a change in the destiny of all humankind." It is with this spirit that members of the SGI pursue their own individual human revolution through their daily Buddhist practice and activities for world peace.

karma—Karma is the accumulation of effects from the good and bad causes that we bring with us from our former lives, as well as from the good and bad causes we have made in this lifetime, which shapes our future. *Karman* is a Sanskrit word that means action. Karma is created by actions—our thoughts, words and deeds—and manifests itself in our appearance, behavior, attitudes, good and bad fortune and where we are born or live. In short—everything about us. It is all the positive and negative influences or causes that make up our complete reality in this world. This law of karmic causality operates in perpetuity, carrying over from one lifetime to the next and remaining with one in the latent state between death and rebirth.

Shakyamuni maintained that what makes a person noble or humble is not birth but one's actions. Therefore the Buddhist doctrine of karma is not fatalistic. Rather, karma is viewed not only as a means to explain the present, but also as the potential force through which to influence one's future. Buddhism therefore encourages people to create the best possible karma in the present in order to ensure the best possible outcome in the future.

Nichiren Buddhism does not consider one's karma or destiny to be fixed since our minds change from moment to moment, even the habitual and destructive tendencies we all possess to varying degrees can be altered. In other words, Buddhism teaches that individuals have within themselves the potential to change their own karma.

Lotus Sutra—This is the twenty-eight-chapter oral teachings, recorded in writing after the death of Shakyamuni, that benefited people during Shakyamuni's lifetime and during the Former Day of the Law.

Whereas Shakyamuni expressed it as the "twenty-eight-chapter Lotus Sutra," Nichiren, to enable all human beings of the Latter Day to attain Buddhahood, revealed the ultimate principle of the Lotus Sutra as Nam-myoho-renge-kyo. The five characters of Myoho-renge-kyo, which constitute the Lotus Sutra's essence—that is Nam-myoho-renge-kyo—are the Lotus Sutra appropriate to this age of the Latter Day of the Law.

The Soka Gakkai's second president, Josei Toda, therefore termed the Daishonin's teaching the Lotus Sutra of the Latter Day.

Since the Lotus Sutra was the central scriptural influence on Nichiren, it is worth mentioning one specific element in it that he thought was crucial. He taught that the Lotus Sutra proclaims that there is an inherent Buddha nature in all human beings. From this comes the idea that all people can attain Buddhahood as they are, as ordinary people in the phenomenal world. This rather revolutionary notion of the essential equality of men and women is central to Nichiren's understanding of the Lotus Sutra and was quite a radical thought at that time in history and in many places in the world even today.

Nam-myoho-renge-kyo—This is the ultimate Law or truth of the universe, according to Nichiren's teaching. Nichiren taught that the essence, all of the benefits of the wisdom contained, in the Lotus Sutra could be realized by chanting its title: [Nam]-myoho-renge-kyo. Chanting these words and excerpts from the Lotus Sutra is the core of this Buddhist practice, supported by study and the sharing of Buddhist teachings.

Namu derives from the Sanskrit word *namas* and is translated as devotion or as dedicating one's life. *Myo* stands for the Dharma nature, or enlightenment, while *ho* represents darkness or ignorance. Together as *myoho*, they express the idea that ignorance and the Dharma nature are a single entity or one in essence. *Renge* stands for the two elements of cause and effect. Cause and effect are also a single entity. *Kyo* represents the words and voices of all living beings. *Kyo* may also be defined as that which is constant and unchanging in the three existences of past, present and future.

Nichiren and Nichiren Buddhism—Nichiren (1222-1282) was the founder of the Buddhist tradition that is based on the Lotus Sutra and urges chanting the phrase Nam-myoho-renge-kyo. Nichiren Buddhism was founded in 1253 in Japan. It is the Buddhism on which the activities of the SGI are based. It places special emphasis on the sanctity of human life and, as a natural outgrowth of this, on world peace. Lasting peace can only be realized by challenging and overcoming the inner impulse toward hatred and violence that exists within all people. Buddhism terms this inner impulse the "fundamental darkness of life." It is the dynamic process of self-reformation through the daily practice of Buddhism that results in the rejuvenation of the individual and society, and forms the core of SGI's vision for a peaceful world.

nine consciousnesses. "Consciousness" is the translation of the Sanskrit *vijnana*, which means discernment. The nine consciousnesses are

(1) sight-consciousness,

(2) hearing-consciousness,

(3) smell-consciousness,

(4) taste-consciousness,

(5) touch-consciousness,

(6) mind-consciousness,

(7) *mano*-consciousness,

(8) *alaya*-consciousness and

(9) *amala*-consciousness.

The first five consciousnesses correspond to the five senses of sight, hearing, smell, taste and touch. The sixth consciousness integrates the perceptions of the five senses into coherent images and makes judgments about the external world.

In contrast to the first six consciousnesses that deal with the external world, the seventh or *mano*-consciousness discerns the inner spiritual world. Awareness of and attachment to the self are said to originate from the *mano*-consciousness, as does the capacity to distinguish between good and evil. The eighth or *alaya*-consciousness is below the level of consciousness. It exists in what modern psychology calls the unconscious. All experiences of the present and previous lifetimes—collectively called karma—are stored there. It receives the *alaya*-consciousness thus forming the framework of individual existence.

The ninth consciousness, the *amala*-consciousness, lies below the *alaya*-consciousness and remains free from all karmic impurity. This ninth consciousness is defined as the basis of all spiritual functions and is identified with the true nature of life. It is the ninth consciousness that we effect when we chant Nam-myoho-renge-kyo.

oneness of life and its environment—This is also referred to as the non-duality of life and its environment. The principle of the oneness of life and its environment describes the inseparable relationship of the individual and the environment. People generally have a tendency to regard the environment as something separate from themselves, and from the viewpoint of that which we can physically observe, we are often justified in drawing this distinction. However, from the viewpoint of ultimate reality, the individual and the environment are one and inseparable. Life manifests itself in both a living subject and an objective environment.

Life indicates a subjective *self* that experiences the karmic effects of past actions. The environment is the objective realm where the karmic effects of life take shape. Environment here does not mean one overall context in which all beings live. Each living being has his or her unique environment in which the effects of karma appear. The effects of one's karma, both good and bad, manifest themselves both in one's self and in the environment, because these are two integral phases of the same entity.

Since both life and its environment are one, whichever of the Ten Worlds an individual manifests internally will be mirrored in his or her environment. Moreover, as people accumulate good karma through Buddhist practice, the effects of that karma will become apparent not only in themselves but also in their environment, in the form of self-awareness, wisdom, improved circumstances, greater respect from others and so forth.

The principle of the oneness of life and its environment is the rationale for asserting that the Buddhist practice of individuals will work a transformation in society. Buddhism expands the entire reality of life and shows the way to live a winning life—the most fulfilled existence.

Shakyamuni (Siddartha Gautama)—Buddhism arose in what is now India about 500 BCE out of the teachings of Shakyamuni, Siddhartha Gautama, also known as the Buddha, "the Enlightened One." Tradition has it that although Gautama's father kept him in princely isolation during his youth, brief glimpses of the pain experienced by ordinary people led him to one of his most fundamental realizations: Life is predicated on suffering and change. This general truth of suffering is emblematically represented in Buddhism as the four sufferings of birth, aging, sickness and death. Confronted with the dilemma of such universal suffering, Shakyamuni, at an early age, decided to renounce his claim to his father's throne and embark on a search for the way to alleviate the pain embodied in these four. After several years of the most extreme form of asceticism, finding himself no closer to an answer, he concluded that the path to understanding that he sought lay neither in asceticism nor in the luxurious life of his youth, but in between them, in a "middle way." Abandoning his ascetic practice and meditating deeply through the night, he destroyed his remaining impurities, eliminated his false views and experienced the goal of Buddhahood.

Thus began the career of one of the great religious figures of history. By all accounts he was a man of boundless compassion and peace. By the time of his death, thousands had been converted to the new wisdom he propounded. Some of those converts joined his monastic order, renouncing the secular world; many did not. After his death, his many teachings were compiled into the twenty-eight chapter Lotus Sutra.

Soka Gakkai International (SGI)— The Soka Gakkai or Value-Creating Society, is a Buddhist lay organization founded in Japan on November 18, 1930, by Tsunesaburo Makiguchi, who became its first president, and his disciple, Josei Toda, its second president. Makiguchi regarded the creation of values that are conducive to a happy life as the purpose of education. In 1928 he encountered the teachings of Nichiren and the Lotus Sutra and found in them resonance with his philosophy of value. Daisaku Ikeda became the third president of the Soka Gakkai in 1960 and is now president of the Soka Gakkai International. The organization has now spread to more than 190 countries and territories with more than twelve million members.

The SGI aims to realize the absolute happiness (enlightenment) of individuals and the prosperity of each country by spreading understanding of the Buddhism of Nichiren Daishonin. Toward that end, the SGI engages in various activities to promote peace, culture and education.

The SGI's membership reflects a broad range of ethnic and social diversity. In the United States, the SGI-USA (*www.sgi-usa.org*) has almost ninety community and activity centers throughout the country. Discussion meetings are conducted monthly in private homes where practicing members and friends study the philosophy and share experiences.

Ten Worlds—These are ten distinct realms or categories of beings referred to in Buddhist scriptures. Loosely defined, from the lowest to the highest these are hell, hunger, animality, anger, humanity, heaven, learning, realization, bodhisattva and Buddhahood. The more accurate translation is the realms of hell, hungry spirits, animals, *asuras,* human beings, heavenly beings, voice-hearers, cause-awakened ones, bodhisattvas and Buddhas. The Ten Worlds were viewed originally as distinct physical locations, each with its own particular inhabitants. The Lotus Sutra, however, teaches that each of the Ten Worlds contains all ten within it, making it possible to interpret them as potential states of life inherent in each individual being. In other words, from the standpoint of the Lotus Sutra, the Ten Worlds indicate ten potential states or conditions that a person can manifest or experience. The mutual possession of the Ten Worlds is a component principle of three thousand realms in a single moment of life, which T'ien-t'ai set forth in *Great Concentration and Insight*.

The Ten Worlds are:

The world of hell. Nichiren's treatise *The Object of Devotion for Observing the Mind* states, "Rage is the world of hell." Hell indicates a condition in which living itself is misery and suffering, and in which, devoid of all freedom, one's anger and rage become a source of further self-destruction.

The world of hungry spirits. This is also called the world of hunger. A condition governed by endless desire for such things as food, profit, pleasure, power, recognition or fame, in which one is never truly satisfied. This world is also characterized by greed.

The world of animals. This is also called the world of animality. It is a condition driven by instinct and a lack of reason, morality or wisdom with which to control oneself. In this condition, one is ruled by the "law of the jungle," standing in fear of the strong, but despising and preying upon those weaker than oneself. The worlds of hell, hungry spirits and animals are collectively known as the three evil paths.

The world of *asuras*. This is also called the world of animosity or the world of anger. In Indian mythology, *asuras* are arrogant and belligerent demons. This condition is called the world of animosity because it is characterized by persistent, though not necessarily overt, aggressiveness. It is a condition dominated by ego, in which excessive pride prevents one from revealing one's true self or seeing others as they really are. The worlds of hell, hungry spirits, animals and *asuras* are collectively called the four evil paths.

The world of human beings. This is also called the world of humanity. In this state, people try to control their desires and impulses with reason and act in harmony with their surroundings and other people, while also aspiring for a higher state of life.

The world of heavenly beings. This is also called the world of heaven or rapture. This is a condition of contentment and joy that one feels when released from suffering or upon satisfaction of some desire. It is a temporary joy that is dependent upon and may easily change with circumstances.

The six worlds from hell through the world of heavenly beings are called the six paths. Beings in the six paths, or those who tend toward these states of life, are largely controlled by the restrictions of their surroundings and are therefore extremely vulnerable to changing circumstances.

The remaining states, in which one transcends the uncertainty of the six paths, are called the four noble worlds:

The world of voice-hearers. This is also called the world of learning. This is a condition in which one awakens to the impermanence of all things and the instability of the six paths. In this state, one dedicates oneself to creating a better life through self-reformation and self-development by learning from the ideas, knowledge and experience of one's predecessors and contemporaries. "Voice-hearers" (Sanskrit *shravaka*) originally meant those who listen to the Buddha preach the four noble truths and practice the eightfold path in order to acquire emancipation from earthly desires.

The world of cause-awakened ones. This is also called the world of realization. It is a condition in which one perceives the impermanence of all phenomena and strives to free oneself from the sufferings of the six paths by seeing some lasting truth through one's own observations and effort. "Cause-awakened ones," also known as "self-awakened ones" (Sanskrit *pratyekabuddha*), originally meant those who attain a form of emancipation by perceiving the twelve-linked chain of causation or by observing natural phenomena. Persons in the worlds of voice-hearers and cause-awakened ones, which are together called persons of the two vehicles, are given more to the pursuit of self-perfection than to altruism. They are also willing to look squarely at the reality of death and seek the eternal, in contrast to those in the world of heaven, who are distracted from life's harsh realities.

The world of bodhisattvas. A state of compassion in which one thinks of and works for others' happiness even before becoming happy oneself. Bodhisattva, which consists of *bodhi* (enlightenment) and *sattva* (beings), means a person who seeks enlightenment while leading others to enlightenment.

Bodhisattvas find that the way to self-perfection lies only in altruism, working for the enlightenment of others even before their own enlightenment. Nichiren states in *The Object of Devotion for Observing the Mind*, "Even a heartless villain loves his wife and children. He, too, has a portion of the bodhisattva world within him."

The world of Buddhas or Buddhahood. This is a state of perfect and absolute freedom in which one realizes the true aspect of all phenomena or the true nature of life. One can achieve this state by manifesting the Buddha nature inherent in one's life. From the standpoint of the philosophy of the mutual possession of the Ten Worlds, Buddhahood should not be viewed as a state removed from the sufferings and imperfections of ordinary persons.

Attaining Buddhahood does not mean becoming a special being. In this state, one still continues to work against and defeat the negative functions of life and transform any and all difficulty into causes for further development. It is a state of complete access to the boundless wisdom, compassion, courage and other qualities inherent in life; with these, one can create harmony with and among others and between human life and nature. Nichiren stated, "Buddhahood is the most difficult to demonstrate," but he also says, "That ordinary people born in the latter age can believe in the Lotus Sutra is due to the fact that the world of Buddhahood is present in the human world."

Previous Buddhist teachers, including Shakyamuni, emphasized a monastic lifestyle. They taught their disciples that the path to enlightenment required detaching themselves from all earthly desires and mastering complex doctrines. Needless to say, this method of achieving enlightenment was only open to a small percentage of society. Most people didn't have the luxury of escaping their daily life. Nichiren, on the other hand, taught his followers that the path to enlightenment was through directly challenging each obstacle in their everyday lives.

Also from Middleway Press

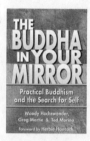

The Buddha in Your Mirror:
Practical Buddhism and the Search for Self,
by Woody Hochswender, Greg Martin
and Ted Morino
(ISBN0-9674697-8-3; $14.00)

Also available in Spanish: *El Buda en Tu*
Espejo
(ISBN 0-9674697-7-5; $14.00)

"Like the Buddha, this book offers practical guidelines to overcome difficulties in everyday life and to be helpful to others.
Readers will find these pages are like a helpful and supportive
friend. I enthusiastically recommend it."

—DR. DAVID CHAPPELL, EDITOR OF
Buddhist Peacework: Creating Cultures of Peace

Choose Hope: Your Role in Waging Peace
in the Nuclear Age by David Krieger and
Daisaku Ikeda

Silver Book of the Year Award, 2003,
ForeWord **Magazine**
(ISBN 0-9674697-6-7; $23.95)

"In this nuclear age, when the future of
humankind is imperiled by irrational strategies, it is impera-
tive to restore sanity to our policies and hope to our destiny.

Only a rational analysis of our problems can lead to their solution. This book is an example par excellence of a rational approach."

—JOSEPH ROTBLAT, NOBEL PEACE PRIZE LAUREATE

For the Sake of Peace: Seven Paths to Global Harmony, A Buddhist Perspective, by Daisaku Ikeda

Winner of the NAPRA Nautilus Award for Social Change 2002
(ISBN 0-9674697-9-1; $14.00)

"At a time when we squander enormous amounts of human and environmental resources on the study of and preparation for making war, *For the Sake of Peace* stands as a primary text in the study and practice of making peace."

—NAPRA, NAUTILUS AWARD CITATION

On Being Human: Where Ethics, Medicine and Spirituality Converge, by Daisaku Ikeda, René Simard and Guy Bourgeault
(ISBN 0-9723267-1-5; $15.95)

"*On Being Human* is an elegant and timely dialogue. Accessible yet profound, it illustrates the convergence of medical science, bioethics and Buddhist philosophy. Informative and hopeful, it offers wise perspectives on life and death, revealing their deeper meaning and higher purpose. Its three sagacious voices speak as one, to all."

— LOU MARINOFF, AUTHOR OF
Plato Not Prozac and *The Big Questions*

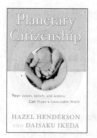

Planetary Citizenship:
Your *Values, Beliefs and Actions*
Can *Shape a Sustainable World*,
by Hazel Henderson and Daisaku Ikeda
(ISBN 0-9723267-2-3; $23.95)

"*Planetary Citizenship* is a delightful introduction to some of the most important
ideas and facts concerning stewardship of
the planet. I cannot think of any book that deals with more
important issues."

— MIHALY CSIKSZENTMIHALYI, AUTHOR OF *Flow:
The Psychology of Optimal Experience*

Soka Education: A Buddhist Vision
for Teachers, Students and Parents,
by Daisaku Ikeda
(ISBN 0-9674697-4-0; $23.95)

From the Japanese word meaning "to create value," this book presents a fresh spiritual perspective to question the ultimate
purpose of education. Mixing American
pragmatism with Buddhist philosophy, the goal of Soka education is the lifelong happiness of the learner.

"[Teachers] will be attracted to Soka and Ikeda's plea that edu-
cators bring heart and soul back to education."

—*Teacher* MAGAZINE

"Ikeda's practical perscription places students' needs first,
empowers teachers, and serves as a framework for global citizenship."

—GEORGE DAVID MILLER, PROFESSOR, LEWIS UNIVERSITY

**Unlocking the Mysteries of Birth &
Death...and Everything in Between:
A Buddhist View of Life (second edition),**
by Daisaku Ikeda
(ISBN 0-9723267-0-7; $15.00)

"In this slender volume, Ikeda presents a
wealth of profound information in a clear
and straightforward style that can be easily
absorbed by the interested lay reader. His life's work, and the
underlying purpose of this book, is simply to help human
beings derive maximum meaning from their lives through the
study of Buddhism."

— ForeWord Magazine

**The Way of Youth: Buddhist Common
Sense for Handling Life's Questions,**
by Daisaku Ikeda
(ISBN 0-9674697-0-8; $14.95)

Also available in Spanish:
A la Manera de los Jóvenes
(ISBN 0-9674697-3-2; $14.95)

"[This book] shows the reader how to
flourish as a young person in the world today; how to build
confidence and character in modern society; learn to live with
respect for oneself and others; how to contribute to a positive,
free and peaceful society; and find true personal happiness."

—Midwest Book Review

*Ask for Middleway Press books at your favorite neighborhood
or On-line bookseller. Or visit www.middlewaypress.com.*

Printed on recycled paper

MIDDLEWAY PRESS is committed to preserving ancient forest and natural resources. We are a member of Green Press Initiative—a nonprofit program dedicated to supporting book publishers in maximizing their use of fiber which is not sourced from ancient or endangered forests. We have elected to print this title on New Leaf EcoBook 100, made with 100% recycled fiber, processed chlorine free. For more information about Green Press Initiative and the use of recycled paper in book publishing, visit www.greenpressinitiative.org.

 NEW LEAF PAPER
ENVIRONMENTAL BENEFITS STATEMENT

Romancing the Buddha is printed on New Leaf EcoBook 100, made with 100% post-consumer waste, processed chlorine free. By using this environmentally friendly paper, the following resources were saved:

trees	water	energy	solid waste	greenhouse gases
45 fully grown	**19,350** gallons	**33** million BTUs	**2,158** pounds	**4,253** pounds

Calculated based on research done by Environmental Defense and other members of the Paper Task Force.

© New Leaf Paper   Visit us in cyberspace at www.newleafpaper.com or call 1-888-989-5323